EDWARDIAN COOKING

The Unofficial
Downton Abbey Cookbook

LARRY EDWARDS

ARCADE PUBLISHING • NEW YORK

Arcade Publishing books may be purchased in bulk at special discounts for sales promotion, corporate gifts, fund-raising, or educational purposes. Special editions can also be created to specifications. For details, contact the Special Sales Department, Arcade Publishing, 307 West 36th Street, 11th Floor, New York, NY 10018 or arcade@skyhorsepublishing.com.

Arcade Publishing® is a registered trademark of Skyhorse Publishing, Inc.®, a Delaware corporation.

Visit our website at www.arcadepub.com.

10 9 8 7 6 5 4 3 2 1

Paperback ISBN: 978-1-62872-316-8

Library of Congress Cataloging-in-Publication Data

Edwards, Larry, 1957– author.
 Edwardian cooking : inspired by Downton Abbey's elegant meals / Larry Edwards.
    pages cm
 ISBN 978-1-61145-778-0 (hardcover : alk. paper) 1. Cooking, English. 2. Cooking—England. I. Title.
 TX717.E4545 2012
 641.5942—dc23
                                    2012025191

Printed in China

Contents

High Tea at the Abbey

The Sweet

The Savory

Dinner at the Abbey

Breads

Soups

Side Dishes

Entrées

Desserts at the Abbey

Introduction

Long before there was the rage of organic food, sustained living, and natural eating, there were the abbeys of Great Britain. Though Downton Abbey is a fictitious abbey, what we see dramatized is very real. From the upstairs/downstairs lifestyles, the separation of classes, and the positions of the people, it is all real. Also very real in the television dramatization is the food.

As opposed to Hollywood versions of the late Victorian era and the Edwardian era, opulence was not the center factor of the dining room. There were never large tables groaning with the weight of culinary fare. As fans of *Downton Abbey* will note, the tables are pretty bare. As a matter of fact, there is never any food on the tables. The food is presented by the footmen to each guest. You never see a golden suckling pig in the middle of a table. You never see large roasts of beef or lamb. You see the table, the linens, the silverware, the service ware, and the glasses.

For the most part, all the food served at the abbeys came from the grounds of the abbeys. On the average, each abbey employed 15 gardeners. These gardeners looked after the vegetable gardens, the fruit orchards, the grazing areas for the animals, and the ponds. All fruit and vegetables were picked the morning before they were prepared. As for the ponds, they were the home to the fish served at the abbey. With very few exceptions, everything served at the abbey was grown at the abbey.

So, what was a typical dinner at the abbey? For the most part, each dinner consisted of three courses. This was elevated to five courses if the guest list featured a member of royalty. The food was prepared by the abbey cook. The cook was assisted by a vegetable maid (who prepped the produce), a stillroom maid (who did the baking), and a scullery maid (responsible for the cookware and bakeware). Other members of the maid staff would plate the food for the footmen to present in the dining room.

Everything that left the kitchen and headed into the dining room was prepared from scratch. The abbey cook would start his/her day at 6 AM. The other kitchen staff members would start at 7 AM. In the course of their 18-hour day, they would prepare eight meals (this includes the meals for the abbey staff). Along with these eight meals, they would also prepare the food for the various High Teas and the numerous social gatherings whether on the grounds of the abbey or in the various sitting rooms.

In preparing and presenting the dishes included within this book, we wanted to be as authentic as possible. During the late-Victorian era and the Edwardian era, the kitchens were run on wood stoves and ovens. Rather obviously, today's kitchens do not have such appliances, so we have adapted the dishes for today's kitchens. As far as the products used in the presented dishes, with very few exceptions, everything is the same.

During the time-span of this book, Europe was engulfed in the horrors of World War I. Due to this, the culinary fare of Great Britain was undergoing a great change and you will notice this in some of the dishes presented. For the first time the national cuisine was being fused with the culinary fare of France and Italy and the reason for this is quite simple. To escape the horrors of the war, many French and Italian citizens were migrating to England. Many of these people were employed by the abbeys as their usual staffs were being drafted or volunteering for the British war efforts.

In keeping with authenticity, we will be presenting the dishes in this book in the same way the dishes would be presented at an abbey. The first section will be dishes served at High Tea—a social gathering featuring more appetizer-type dishes. This section will be separated into sweet and savory.

The section entitled Dinner at the Abbey will be presented just as they were by the footmen serving the guests. You will have the Breads of the Abbey, Soups of the Abbey, and then the side dishes and the entrées.

As with any meal prepared and served at the abbeys, dinner will be followed by the Desserts of the Abbey. The desserts served at the abbey were usually very simple and mostly very rich. They were meant to end the evening on a sweet note, not weigh the guests down.

Each of the included recipes were kitchen- and taste-tested personally by Chef Larry Edwards. For each dish you will have a photograph of the finished product. None of these photographs have been altered in any shape, way, or form. No color enhancements have been used. What you see is exactly what you will make and present.

Celebrate the magic and majesty of the food inspired by *Downton Abbey* and enjoy the royal fare from Edwardian England!

High Tea
at the Abbey

❖ ❖ ❖

The Sweet

English Rum Balls

(serving amount depends on size)

Like any other home, the abbey had a kitchen budget. The cook was always alert to being frugal. These cookies are a result of being frugal. The base of the confection is day-old shortbread. At Downton Abbey, the perfect day-old shortbread to be used would be the King Edward Coronation Toffee Shortbread (see the recipe in this section). They can also be prepared using commercially produced shortbread, however the richness and taste will be altered.

To many, this confection may look reminiscent to the holiday American cookie known as Bourbon Balls. The difference here, aside from the liquor used, is that this Edwardian version is much more suited to the palate. It has a lighter density due to the use of the short-bread and the sweetness is slightly abated due to the use of powdered sugar.

Once these are prepared, they should be stored in an airtight container and dusted with granulated sugar daily. At the abbey, these would be served a week after they had been prepared (they do not go bad due to the amount of rum used).

Ingredients needed to make English Rum Balls:

2 cups crushed day-old shortbread cookies

¾ cup powdered sugar

1 cup finely ground walnuts

2 Tbs. dark cocoa powder, unsweetened

¼ cup rum

⅓ cup light corn syrup

granulated sugar (for dusting the cookies with)

Steps:

1. In a large bowl, combine all of the ingredients and mix until moist and blended.

2. Remove walnut-sized portions of the mixture and roll into a ball.

3. Roll the balls in some granulated sugar.

4. Place the balls into an air-tight container. Sprinkle with some more sugar. Place the lid on the container and let sit in dark and dry place until ready to serve.

High Tea Finger Cookies

(serving amount depends on size)

If you have watched *Downton Abbey,* you are well aware that protocol played a big part in life at an abbey. Of all the dishes prepared at an abbey, it is these "biscuits" ("cookies" in America) that had to follow a strict presentation protocol. Each of the biscuits had to be exactly two inches in length, thus their name of finger cookies (the two inches being the average equivalent of the first two joints of a finger).

High Tea, or social gatherings, at the abbey were often segregated events. For the most part, men were served savory items and the women sweet. These biscuits were always served where the women gathered. Though the recipe is quite simple, to properly present them is not as simple. Due to the delicate crumb of this biscuit, they must be cut as soon as they are taken from the oven. If you wait more than a few minutes, they will crumble under the pressure of the knife.

When presented, High Tea Finger Cookies were always accompanied by small bowls of fresh fruit preserves (one of which was always a marmalade) and a coddled or Devonshire cream, which would often be spread upon the biscuit.

Ingredients needed to make High Tea Finger Cookies:

3½ cups flour

1 Tbs. baking powder

1 cup sugar

1 cup butter, softened

3 whole eggs

1 tsp. vanilla

heavy cream for brushing

Steps:

1. Preheat the oven to 350°F and line a baking sheet with parchment paper or a silicon sheet.

2. In a medium bowl, whisk the flour and baking powder.

3. In a mixer with a paddle attachment, cream the butter and sugar until smooth and pale.

4. Beat in the eggs and vanilla until smooth.

5. Add the flour mixture and beat until a soft dough is formed.

6. Pour the dough into a pastry bag fitted with a large round tip.

7. Pipe long strands of the dough onto the prepared baking sheet.

8. Brush the dough with some heavy cream.

9. Place into the oven and bake 20 minutes.

10. Remove from the oven and immediately cut into two-inch fingers.

11. Remove the cookies from the sheet and let cool on a rack until ready to serve.

Tea Cake Cookies

(makes 16)

Whereas women had special dishes for High Tea and social gatherings, so did their male counterparts. This particular biscuit (cookie) was created to go along with a stronger blend of tea (as well as black coffee) and prepared in a bigger size to better suit the larger hands of a male. They were also made less sweet, as the men would often smoke cigars and a less sweet taste would not distract from the taste of the cigar.

When presenting these at special events, the shape of these cookies would often be the crest of the family who owned the abbey. At times when this was not thought to be necessary, they were simply molded into a small tart pan and as soon as they were taken from the oven, they were cut into quarters.

For fans of *Downton Abbey*, you might recall that often times in the bedrooms and guestrooms, the maids refer to the "biscuit jars" on the bedside table. The biscuits, which would be in those jars, are this recipe, albeit they were prepared smaller and in a round shape.

Ingredients needed to make Tea Cake Cookies:

¼ cup butter, softened

¾ cup sugar

2 eggs

2 cups flour

1 tsp. baking powder

¼ cup cream

Steps:

1. Preheat the oven to 350°F. Lightly oil the bottom and sides of four small tart pans.

2. In a mixer with a paddle attachment, cream the butter, sugar, and eggs until smooth.

3. Add the flour, baking powder, and cream, and beat just until the dough starts to come together. Do not over beat as you will lose the consistency of the cookie.

4. Divide the dough into quarters. Mold each quarter into the prepared tart pans.

5. Place the tart pans onto a baking sheet and place into the oven.

6. Bake the cookies 20 minutes, or until the edges begin to pull away from the pan.

7. Remove the cookies from the oven and carefully remove them from the tart pans.

8. Cut the cookies into quarters and let cool on a rack until ready to serve.

Scottish Shortbread

(makes 6 small tarts)

The basic protocol for dishes served for High Tea was no more than a two-bite portion. When it came to the classic Scottish Shortbread, it was permissible to shy away from protocol. This was one of the few dishes of High Tea served upon a plate and with a fork and knife.

Scottish Shortbread was a favorite sweet served to both genders, yet it was served different ways to each. When served to the woman, it was often drizzled with triple cream, which would make the shortbread more moist and easier to cut into. For the men, it would usually be served with a simple dusting of powdered sugar.

The cooks at the abbey loved to prepare this dish as it was very simple and took no time. What was not so simple was its removal from the tart pan. This may very well be one of the most delicate pastries one can prepare. Due to the fact it is held together only with butter, the crumb is satiny smooth and can actually almost break apart when blown upon. For today's cook, it is highly recommended that you use a tart pan with a removable bottom.

Ingredients needed to make Scottish Shortbread:

1½ cups flour

½ cup cornstarch

½ cup sugar

1 cup butter, chilled and diced

Steps:

1. Preheat the oven to 350°F and lightly oil the bottom and sides of six small tart pans.

2. In a medium bowl, whisk together the flour, cornstarch, and sugar until blended.

3. Add the chilled and diced butter, using a pastry blender or pastry fork to cut the butter into the flour mixture until it resembles crumbs.

4. Spoon the crumble mixture into the prepared tart pans and pat it down with your finger tips.

5. Place the tart pans onto a baking sheet and place into the oven.

6. Bake 35 minutes.

7. Remove the shortbreads from the oven.

8. Remove the shortbreads from the tart pans and let cool on a rack until ready to serve.

Apricot Crowned Jewels

(makes 24)

Always one of the highlights of any High Tea at any abbey were these little pastries of immense richness and melt-in-your-mouth goodness. Created using a slightly sweetened cream cheese dough, rolled in coarsely ground almonds and crowned with a fresh apricot preserve, these were the focal point of aristocratic goodness.

The lush orchards of the Edwardian abbeys were know for their bountiful harvests of fresh fruits. One of the favorite fruits were apricots. To make their apricot preserves, the cooks would use very ripe apricots and chop them finely. They would then add them to a pot with some lemon juice and sugar and cook it down to a spreading consistency. For today's cook, it is easier to buy a small jar of high-quality apricot preserves.

It is believed that the American cookie called Tom Thumbs is an adaptation of this Edwardian classic. This may be true, however the cooks at the abbey used their index finger to make the crevice to hold the apricot preserves and to make sure the crevice was neat and even, with each cookie they dipped their finger into cold water.

Ingredients needed to make Apricot Crowned Jewels:

1¾ cups flour

¼ tsp. salt

1 pkg. cream cheese (8 ounces), softened

1 cup butter

¼ cup sugar

coarsely ground almonds for rolling

apricot preserves for crowning

Steps:

1. Preheat the oven to 350°F. Line a baking sheet with parchment paper or a silicon sheet.

2. In a medium bowl, whisk the flour and salt.

3. In a mixer with a paddle attachment, beat the cream cheese, butter, and sugar until combined.

4. Add the flour and beat until it forms a soft dough.

5. Place the dough into the refrigerator and chill 30 minutes.

6. Remove walnut-size portions of the dough and roll into a ball.

7. Roll the dough into the coarsely ground almonds and place on the prepared baking sheet.

8. Using your index finger, make an indentation in the middle of each ball and fill with some apricot preserves.

9. Place into the oven and bake 15 minutes.

10. Remove from the oven and let cool on a wire rack until ready to serve.

High Tea Lemon Butter Biscuits

(makes 18)

Though Downton Abbey is a fictitious abbey, the situations therein are all factually true. There was the aristocratic upstairs and the lower caste downstairs. Though most of the families did indeed care about their staff, there was very little mingling between the two and very seldom the sharing of the same types of food. In the case of High Tea Lemon Butter Biscuits, the families would usually allow portions to be made for the staff on special days. The reason these treats were considered special is the fact citrus fruit was very hard to come by in Great Britain during the Edwardian era and when available, cost a great deal of money.

These delicious pastries are considered one of the classic of the High Tea biscuits (cookies). As most tea drinkers know, there is a wonderful taste marriage between lemon and tea. As with most of the High Tea pastries, these are only slightly sweetened and they get their lemony aura not from the juice of the lemon, but from the finely grated zest (yellow portion of the rind).

During the Christmas holidays at the abbey, these cookies would be served at every social event with one slight difference. During Christmas they would always be served with a lemon glaze as an extra added lemony treat.

Ingredients needed to make High Tea Lemon Butter Biscuits:

1 cup flour	1 lemon, zest only and finely grated
2 Tbs. cornstarch	½ cup butter
½ tsp. salt	¼ cup sugar
1 tsp. baking powder	1 egg yolk

Steps:

1. Preheat the oven to 375°F and line a baking sheet with parchment paper or a silicon sheet.

2. In a medium bowl, whisk together the flour, cornstarch, salt, baking powder, and lemon zest.

3. In a mixer with a paddle attachment, beat the butter, sugar, and egg yolk until pale and creamy.

4. Stir, do not beat, the flour mixture into the butter mixture just until blended.

5. Pinch off walnut-size portions of the dough and roll into a ball.

6. Place the cookies on the prepared pan and place into the oven.

7. Bake 15 minutes.

8. Remove the pan from the oven and let the cookies cool on the pan 5 minutes.

9. Remove the cookies to a wire rack to cool until ready to serve.

Victoria Tea Cookies

(makes 36)

Legend has it that these were Queen Victoria's favorite cookie. So in love was her majesty with these cookies that wherever she was present, there were to be trays of these cookies available to her. During the late Victorian era and into the Edwardian era, these treats became a staple at High Tea as an honor to her monarchy.

As opposed to the usual biscuits and cookies presented at High Tea and social gatherings, Victoria Tea Cookies do take a little more work and preparation. They are a feathery light cookie and they require the batter to be aired out by folding in egg white. When prepared today, they have a slight aura of vanilla. During the Edwardian era and at the abbeys, this flavor aura was due to the use of almond extract.

It is said that Queen Victoria liked to dip her cookie in triple cream before placing it upon her tongue. This is the reason platters of these cookies were always presented around a bowl of either triple or Devonshire cream. For today's kitchen, they would be served with a bowl of slightly sweetened whipped cream. It should be noted these cookies will only keep fresh for the day they are baked.

Ingredients needed to make Victoria Tea Cookies:

3 eggs, separated

2 Tbs. sugar

1 tsp. almond extract

½ cup flour

powdered sugar for dusting

Steps:

1. Preheat the oven to 350°F. Line a baking sheet with parchment paper or a silicon sheet.

2. In a mixer with a paddle attachment, beat the egg yolks, sugar, and almond extract until the mixture thickens and becomes pale. This will take a few minutes and is important to the final texture of the cookie.

3. Sift the flour over the batter and don't do anything else. Do not stir or fold the flour into the batter. This is important for the texture of the cookies.

4. Whisk the eggs white until stiff peaks form.

5. Fold the egg whites into the batter, at the same type you will be incorporating the flour. This will lighten the batter and give it body.

6. Spoon the mixture into a pastry bag fitted with a plain round tip.

7. Pipe the batter through the tip making little mounds. Give each cookie about an inch of space between themselves.

8. Place into the oven and bake 10 minutes.

9. Remove the cookies from the oven and let cool on the pan 5 minutes.

10. Remove the cookies from the pan to a wire rack, dust with powdered sugar and let cool until ready to serve.

CREAM SCONES

(makes 8 wedges)

One of the most famous British culinary imports to the world is the pastry known as scones. This popular breakfast fare has many variation but none quite like this version for the very simple reason, these are not the breakfast type! These scones were originated specifically for High Teas. Whereas the typical scones are thick and usually sliced in half for presentation, these are much thinner and the only liquid involved is heavy cream (un-whipped whipping cream).

When High Tea Cream Scones were served at the abbey's High Tea, they were always accompanied by four spreads. Two of these spreads were fruit preserves and the others were butter and triple or Devonshire cream.

It is highly recommended that the scones be cut into wedges at soon as they are taken from the oven. Due to the fact the only liquid used within the recipe is heavy cream, the crumb of this scone is very fragile.

Ingredients needed to make High Tea Cream Scones:

2 cups flour

1 Tbs. baking powder

¼ cup sugar

1 tsp. salt

5 Tbs. butter, chilled and diced

1 cup heavy cream

Steps:

1. Preheat the oven to 425°F. Line the bottom of an 8-inch round cake pan with parchment paper.

2. In a medium bowl, whisk together the flour, baking powder, sugar, and salt.

3. Add the chilled butter to the bowl and using a pastry blender or pastry fork, cut the butter into the flour until it resembles crumbs.

4. Stir in the heavy cream into the dough until blended.

5. Place the dough onto a floured surface and using your hands, work the dough until it comes together.

6. Place the dough into the prepared pan and pat it down and even it out.

7. Place into the oven and bake 15 minutes.

8. Remove from the oven and invert (turn over) the pan onto a wire rack.

9. Cut the scones into eight wedges and let cool until ready to serve.

King Edward Coronation Toffee
Shortbread
(makes 8 wedges)

To celebrate the coronation of King Edward and the birth of the Edwardian era throughout Great Britain, a new pastry was created. As with most, if not all, dishes to celebrate the monarchy, there was a hint of the past involved. One of Queen Victoria's favorite sweets was what is referred to as English Toffee. The new Edwardian era was to be a time of renewed wealth for Great Britain (which failed to happen due to World War I). This pastry blended these two eras.

The first time this pastry was served was during the various parties to celebrate the coronation of King Edward. After the coronation and to pay homage to his majesty, the pastry became a regular table feature at High Teas throughout the various abbeys of England. Its original presentation to guests was as slivered (very thinly sliced) wedges. This was due to the incredible richness of the pastry. Now, when served, it is more of a dessert feature; a thick wedge served with a dollop of whipped cream.

When the cooks of the abbey made this dish, they used raw sugar. We have adapted this recipe for today's kitchen, thus the inclusion of brown sugar.

Ingredients needed to make King Edward Coronation Toffee Shortbread:

1 cup butter, softened
2 egg yolks
1 cup brown sugar

1 Tbs. vanilla
2 cups flour

Steps:

1. Preheat the oven to 350°F. Line an 8-inch round cake pan with parchment paper.

2. In a mixer with the paddle attachment, beat the butter, egg yolks, brown sugar, and vanilla until smooth.

3. Add the flour and beat on a low speed until well combined.

4. Place the dough into the prepared pan and press into place with your fingertips.

5. Place into the oven and bake 25 minutes.

6. Remove from the oven and let cool in the pan 10 minutes.

7. Remove from the pan, cut into wedges, and let cool on a wire rack until ready to serve.

Dainty Ladies

(makes 32 small cookies)

A staple of the drawing rooms and salons that served High Tea, these sweet sensations truly lived up to their feminine name. Served primarily to the female guests, Dainty Ladies are very buttery rich and have a wonderful texture, all of which was created to accentuate the taste of tea.

When Dainty Ladies appeared on the table, the guests knew something special was about to happen. This is one of only a few dishes of the Edwardian era to feature coconut and the reason for this is rather simple. Obviously, you couldn't grow coconut anywhere in Great Britain. It had to be imported at great cost. When (and if) an abbey had coconut, it was locked up with only the butler of the house having the key.

You might have noticed when watching *Downton Abbey* that quite often during High Tea or a social gathering featuring food, the women would wear white gloves. If Dainty Ladies were one of the featured sweets, the footman presenting the cookie would inform the guest and the guest would remove here right glove and with her thumb and forefinger, retrieve a cookie. The reason for this is the amount of butter used to make Dainty Ladies would soil the gloves.

Ingredients needed to make Dainty Ladies:

2 cups flour

1 cup flaked coconut

1 cup rolled oats (oatmeal)

1 tsp. baking soda

2 tsp. cream of tartar

1 cup butter

1 Tbs. corn syrup

2 Tbs. water

1 Tbs. vanilla

Steps:

1. Preheat the oven to 325°F. Line the bottom of a baking sheet with parchment paper or a silicon sheet.

2. In a large bowl, whisk together the flour, coconut, rolled oats, baking soda, and cream of tartar.

3. In a small pan over medium heat, melt the butter into the corn syrup and water. Once the butter has melted, stir in the vanilla.

4. Pour the butter mixture into the flour mixture and stir until it is combined.

5. Let the dough sit 5 minutes for the oats to soak up the butter mixture.

6. Remove walnut-size portions of the mixture and roll into a ball.

7. Place the balls onto the prepared baking sheet.

8. Place into the oven and bake 12 minutes.

9. Remove from the oven and place the cookies on a wire rack to cool.

Brown Sugar Honey Balls

(makes 24)

Whereas Dainty Ladies were the epitome of the feminine biscuit (cookie), their counterpart would have to be Brown Sugar Honey Balls. These globular buttery rich sweets are more dense, slightly more sweet, and tinged with the taste of toffee. For the most part, these were served in the library or the study, two of the most common places for the men to celebrate High Tea with one another.

When the cooks of the abbeys would prepare Brown Sugar Honey Balls, they would roll the dough into balls using oil covered hands. This was done for two reasons: First, the dough is a little sticky and it was less of a mess. Secondly, it gave the balls a slight outer moisture so that when they were dredged (coated) with the raw sugar, the sugar would adhere to the dough.

On very rare occasions, usually only major holidays, each of these cookies would be dipped in brandy before being placed on a serving platter and being presented.

Ingredients needed to make Brown Sugar Honey Balls:

1 cup butter, softened

⅔ cup brown sugar

1 Tbs. honey

1 Tbs. vanilla

2⅓ cups flour

1 tsp. baking powder

raw sugar for dredging

Steps:

1. Preheat the oven to 325°F. Line a baking sheet with parchment paper or a silicon sheet.

2. In a mixer with the paddle attachment, add the butter, brown sugar, honey, and vanilla and beat until smooth.

3. Into the mixer add the flour and baking powder and beat until a stiff dough is formed.

4. Remove walnut-size portions of the dough and roll into balls.

5. Dredge (coat) each ball in the raw sugar.

6. Place on the prepared cookie sheet.

7. Place into the oven and bake 20 minutes.

8. Remove from the oven. Place the balls onto a wire rack to cool until ready to serve.

Abbey Banana Walnut Bread

(makes 1 loaf)

One of the more popular sweet types of breads to come out of Great Britain is the classic banana bread. There are a myriad of variations of this bread but one of the tastiest and moistest is a version that was very popular during the Edwardian era and a very popular High Tea specialty.

This version contains the two popular spices of the era, nutmeg and cinnamon. As with many of the sweet variety of dishes, it was also sweetened with brown sugar, thus giving the bread a richer look and flavor. The incredible moistness of this bread comes from the inclusion of olive oil—there is no butter in this recipe! You might also notice that whole wheat flour is used. This was a very common practice at the abbeys as whole wheat flour was less expensive than the processed and dyed white flour.

It is interesting to note that when there was leftover bread, the cooks would toast it and serve it to the staff for their morning meals. When this bread is toasted, it takes on a whole new and absolutely delicious flavor.

Ingredients needed to make Abbey Banana Walnut Bread:

2¼ cups whole wheat flour

2 tsp. baking powder

1 tsp. baking soda

½ tsp. salt

½ tsp. ground cinnamon

½ tsp. ground nutmeg

3 bananas, peeled and mashed

¾ cup brown sugar

¾ cup olive oil

1 egg, beaten

2 tsp. vanilla

1 cup finely chopped walnuts

Steps:

1. Preheat the oven to 350°F. Line the bottom of a 9 × 5 loaf pan with parchment paper.

2. In a large bowl, whisk together the wheat flour, baking powder, baking soda, salt, cinnamon, and nutmeg.

3. In a mixer with the whisk attachment, beat the bananas, brown sugar, olive oil, egg, and vanilla until smooth and creamy. This will take a few minutes as you want the banana to break down.

4. Add the flour mixture and beat on low speed until a batter is formed.

5. Stir in the walnuts.

6. Spoon the batter into the prepared pan.

7. Place into the oven and bake 50 minutes (or until the sides break away from the pan).

8. Remove from the oven and let the bread cool in the pan 15 minutes.

9. Remove from the pan to a wire rack and let cool until ready to slice and serve.

Treacle Cookies

(makes 12 large cookies)

When it came to holidays such as Christmas at the abbeys there was always one cookie that was the star attraction. So popular were these cookies that the house staff also had a small plate placed on the bedside tables in all the guestrooms. These were also a cookie that were readily available for the downstairs staff as well. Rich in taste, dark in color, and flavored with spices, Treacle Cookies are a British classic!

This recipe for Treacle Cookies has been adapted for today's kitchen. Due to the fact that treacle is not easy to find in most parts of the world, we adapted the recipe to replace the treacle with molasses. The texture and spiciness of the cookie remains the same. The taste differs slightly as treacle has a minor bitterness to it.

Of particular interest here is how the abbey cook would go about the final preparation for this cookie. To get the appealing look to the cookie, the cook would dip the dough into heavy cream and then dredge it in powdered sugar.

Ingredients needed to make Treacle Cookies:

¾ cup shortening (do not substitute butter)

1 cup brown sugar

¼ cup molasses

1 egg

2 tsp. fresh ground ginger

2¼ cups flour

2 tsp. baking soda

1 tsp. ground cinnamon

½ tsp. salt

heavy cream for dipping

powdered sugar for dredging (coating)

Steps:

1. Preheat the oven to 375°F. Line a baking sheet with parchment paper or a silicon sheet.

2. In a mixer with a paddle attachment, beat the shortening and brown sugar until smooth.

3. Add the molasses, egg, and ground ginger and beat until well incorporated (at least 4 minutes).

4. In a medium bowl, whisk together the flour, baking soda, ground cinnamon, and salt.

5. With the mixer on a slow speed, add the dry ingredients ½ cup at a time. Beat until you have a firm dough.

6. Remove golf ball-size portions of the dough and roll into a ball.

7. Dip the balls into some heavy cream and then dredge (coat) with the powdered sugar.

8. Place on the prepared baking sheet, leaving at least two inches for the cookies to spread.

9. Place into the oven and bake 10 to 15 minutes.

10. Remove from the oven and let the cookies cool on the baking sheet 5 minutes.

11. Remove the cookie and place on a wire rack to cool.

The Savory

PICKLED FETA CHEESE

(serves 4)

You've seen it on *Downton Abbey*. You've seen it in films that depict the Victorian and Edwardian era. You've seen it in *Upstairs/Downstairs*. The footmen or maids deliver platters of cheese to men and women celebrating High Tea. This is one of those cheese dishes. A savory delight that was served alongside water crackers and thinly sliced bread.

All of the abbeys had wonderful herb gardens and the cooks would always love to include these herbs in their dishes. This very simple savory appetizer uses four different herbs, each one chosen to bring out the taste of the feta cheese. You will notice the use of cayenne peppers in this dish. Though not a common spice during the Edwardian era, it was indeed a staple of the abbey kitchen and used more for its color than its spicy heat.

Aside from Pickled Feta Cheese being a very popular savory High Tea dish, it was also a favorite at all garden parties, picnics, and in the box seats of the famed polo matches.

Ingredients needed to make Pickled Feta Cheese:

½ pound feta cheese

2 tsp. red wine vinegar

2 Tbs. extra virgin olive oil

¼ tsp. ground cayenne pepper

½ tsp. minced tarragon

½ tsp. minced thyme

½ tsp. minced rosemary

1 tsp. minced mint

Steps:

1. Slice the feta cheese into ¼-inch slices and place on a chilled serving platter.

2. In a small bowl, whisk together the remaining ingredients.

3. Drizzle the dressing over the cheese, cover with plastic wrap and chill at least 1 hour before serving.

4. Remove from the refrigerator, unwrap and let sit 1 hour at room temperature before serving.

DEEP-FRIED RYE BREAD

(serves 4)

Probably the most famous bread to ever come out of Great Britain is their famed rye bread. A dark and rich bread of wondrous fresh taste and often served with savory spreads at both dinner and High Tea. This particular version of rye bread was the creation of the kitchen cooks of the Edwardian era. Perhaps it came about as a way of using leftover rye bread dough or maybe they just got tired of kneading the dough to make the bread. Regardless of the reason, it is original and quite delicious.

This dish was served to the men during their High Tea and social gatherings. There are no records of it ever being served to the women and the reason for this may be that deep-fried foods would soil their hands and their gloves. Another reason may be that the bread had to be broken open (not a dainty procedure for a woman) and then a savory spread was delicately added to each piece.

You will notice that as opposed to the rye breads of today, this features no caraway seeds. There are other lighter rye breads of the era that do feature the seeds but because this version of rye bread was deep-fried and not baked, the thought was the essential oils from the seeds (which offers the bread their taste) would not favor the high heat of the frying.

Ingredients needed to make Deep-Fried Rye Bread:

1 cup flour

1 cup rye flour

1 tsp. salt

1 tsp. ground cinnamon

1 tsp. baking powder

1 egg, beaten

2 tsp. dark molasses

1 cup milk

vegetable oil for deep-frying

Steps:

1. In a medium bowl, whisk together the flour, rye flour, salt, cinnamon, and baking powder.

2. In a small bowl, whisk together the egg and molasses until well combined.

3. Stir the egg mixture into the flour until moistened. Stir in the milk to form a stiff batter.

4. In a deep-fryer or a large sauté pan, add enough oil to deep-fry and bring it to 360°F on a deep-fry thermometer.

5. Using a tablespoon, carefully drop portions of the batter into hot oil and deep-fry until golden brown.

6. Remove from the oil with a slotted spoon and let drain on paper towels before serving.

BAKED STUFFED MUSHROOMS

(serves 4)

If you have watched *Downton Abbey*, you are well aware of the fact the abbey was often visited by dignitaries and royalty. On these occasions very special dishes were presented both at the dinners and the High Teas. One of these High Tea specialties was baked mushrooms. Freshly harvested mushrooms from the grounds of the abbey were stuffed with herbs and smoked meat and given a very special touch with imported anchovies.

It was this type of dish that would often send the abbey cook into a frenzy. Due to the fact it was being prepared for a dignitary, it had to be perfect. If not, the cook could lose his/her position. The cook and his/her staff were dealing with products they weren't used to and a preparation they were not accustomed to. If everything went perfect, the cook would often be rewarded with an extra half-day off.

This recipe has been adapted from the original recipe for the simple reason, Chef Larry Edwards couldn't decipher one of the original recipes given to him. Some of the products needed were not available within the United States and the cooking method in the original recipe was for a wood burning oven.

Ingredients needed to make Baked Stuffed Mushrooms:

¼ cup fresh bread crumbs

¼ cup heavy cream

1 pound medium-size mushrooms

2 porcini mushrooms, coarsely chopped

½ cup chopped pancetta (Italian cured meat)

4 anchovy fillets

1 Tbs. minced basil

1 clove garlic, minced

1 egg, beaten

3 Tbs. minced parsley

⅓ tsp. minced marjoram

½ cup dry bread crumbs

⅓ cup extra virgin olive oil

Steps:

1. In a small bowl, combine the fres[h] breadcrumbs and the cream. Set the bowl aside.

2. Remove the stems from the mushrooms. Set the stems and the caps of the mushroom aside.

3. Preheat the oven to 400°F.

4. In a food processor, place the porcini mushrooms, the mushroom stems, pancetta, and anchovies and puree. Spoon the puree into a bowl and stir in the basil and garlic. Set the bowl aside.

5. Squeeze the fresh bread crumbs with your hands of any excess cream and stir it into the puree along with the egg, parsley and marjoram.

6. Rub some oil into an ovenproof baking dish. Place the mushroom caps into the prepared dish and fill the caps with the puree.

7. Sprinkle the dried bread crumbs over the stuffed mushrooms and drizzle them with the remaining olive oil.

8. Place the mushrooms into the oven and bake 30 minutes.

9. Remove from the oven, place on a serving platter, and serve.

Herring Balls

(makes 24)

During the Edwardian era, Herring Balls were a very popular dish among both classes of Englanders. For the lower caste, they were made with either a pickled or creamed herring. For the aristocrats, it was a salted herring. Herring at the abbeys were brought in fresh and the cook would do the salting (preserving) him/herself.

When Herring Balls were requested by either the lord or the lady of the abbey, the procedure of preparation began 24 hours before the dish was to be served. The salted herring had to soak overnight in cold water. Due to the fact refrigeration was not used at the abbeys, a member of the kitchen staff had to change the water every hour.

Chances are very strong that today's cook does not salt their own herring. You can buy salted herring at most Jewish markets or kosher delicatessens. You can also prepare this dish using fresh, pickled, or creamed herring, with no other alteration of the recipe. If, per chance, you can't find salted herring, you may use salted cod fillets.

Ingredients needed to make Herring Balls:

2 salted herring fillets

1 cup cold mashed potatoes

½ pound ground beef or lamb

1 Tbs. flour

¼ tsp. ground black pepper

¼ cup cream

¼ cup butter

Steps:

1. If using salted herring, fill a large bowl with cold water, add the salted herring and let soak overnight in the refrigerator.

2. Remove the fish from the water and pat dry. Discard the soaking water.

3. Remove any bones that might be in the fish and discard. Finely chop the fish.

4. In a medium bowl combine all the ingredients, except the butter, and mix well.

5. Pinch off walnut-size pieces of the fish mixture and roll into balls. Set them aside 10 minutes to rest.

6. In a medium sauté pan or skillet, melt the butter over medium heat. Add the herring balls and brown on all sides.

7. Remove the herring balls with a slotted spoon and place on paper towels to drain of any excess oil.

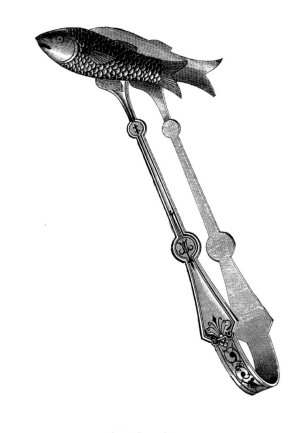

Iced Camembert

(serves 4)

When this dish was listed on the High Tea menu, it was listed as "Camembert de Normandie," as the abbeys used real Camembert cheese, which is made with unpasteurized milk. Today, outside of Europe, this actual Camembert cheese is hard to find due to FDA rules and regulations regarding unpasteurized milk products. Though Camembert cheese was a French product, it became very popular in Great Britain after the end of World War I.

Though this dish was very popular fare for the High Tea gatherings of both sexes, it was mostly preferred by the women due to its delicate flavor and spreadable manageability. More times than not, this dish would be presented with fresh crumpets (see crumpet recipe in this section) or English popovers (see English Popover recipe in this section). When this dish is served today, it is usually accompanied by water crackers or points (crustless triangles) of bread.

For the ultimate in taste and spreadable texture, after freezing the dish it must be thawed at least one hour before presenting at the table.

Ingredients needed to make Iced Camembert:

8 ounces Camembert cheese

¼ cup dry white wine

¼ cup heavy cream

¼ tsp. cayenne pepper

2 Tbs. dry bread crumbs

¼ cup grated Parmesan cheese

½ tsp. sweet paprika

Steps:

1. Add the Camembert cheese, dry white wine, heavy cream, cayenne pepper, and bread crumbs into a food processor, and puree.

2. Line a 6-inch tart pan with parchment paper or use a tart pan with a removable bottom.

3. Spoon the pureed cheese into the prepared tart pan.

4. Sprinkle the top with the Parmesan cheese and paprika.

5. Cover with plastic wrap and freeze two hours.

6. Remove from the freezer and let thaw (soften) one hour.

7. Remove the Iced Camembert from the tart pan, place on a serving platter and serve.

GRANTHAM FAMILY CRUMPETS

(makes 12 depending on size)

In the days of the family-owned abbeys, all the families had their own version of a crumpet. Because Downton Abbey is a fictionalized Abbey, Chef Larry Edwards adapted a typical English crumpet recipe and gave it its own distinctive quality. In doing so, he has named it after the family of Downton Abbey, Grantham Family Crumpets.

So, what really is a crumpet? In all actuality it is what today would be called an English muffin, yet with more taste and character. It is a rather strange batter, very liquidly and gooey, which is the reason the finished dish has the characteristic holes throughout its body. At the abbeys, these were baked in the wood-burning ovens on bricks with the batter being in crumpet rings. For today's kitchen, you can spoon the batter into biscuit or egg rings and cook them on a griddle.

In presenting the crumpet, the footman would slice around the crumpet (not through it) and then gently separate the two sides, once again, just as if it was an English muffin. The crumpets would be served with butter, fruit preserves, Devonshire cream, or various savory spreads.

Ingredients needed to make Grantham Family Crumpets:

2 tsp. yeast

1 Tbs. honey

2¾ cups warm water

3 cups flour

1½ tsp. salt

1 tsp. baking soda

2 Tbs. cold water

oil for brushing the griddle

Steps:

1. In a small bowl, whisk the yeast, sugar, and 1 cup of warm water. Let the mixture stand 5 minutes to proof (foam).

2. In a large bowl, whisk together the flour, salt, and baking soda.

3. Stir the proofed yeast and remaining 1¾ cups warm water into the flour.

4. Cover the bowl with a lint-free towel and let rest one hour. The batter will become very bubbly and gaseous.

5. Stir the cold water into the batter and let it rest 15 minutes.

6. Preheat a griddle or griddle pan over medium heat.

7. Brush the griddle with some oil.

8. Place the empty biscuit or egg rings on the griddle and with a spoon, fill them halfway with the batter (they will rise).

9. Cook the crumpets about 4 minutes on one side and 2 minutes on the other side.

10. Remove the crumpets from the pan and the rings and let cool on a wire rack until ready to serve.

ENGLISH POPOVERS

(makes 6)

There are two basic types of popovers: French popovers and English popovers. From a taste and texture perspective, there is very little difference. From a visual perspective, they are night and day. Whereas a French popover has a smooth top, the English version is meant to have a top that resembles a crown. Aside from being a very popular breakfast treat at the abbeys, they were also a staple at almost every High Tea.

For those unaccustomed to a popover, they are a very light pastry that resembles a muffin-like product from the outside. The magic, however, of the popover is the inside. There is nothing. It is a hollow shell, meant to be filled with a fruit compote or a savory spread. A few of the most common savory spreads for a popover can be found in the next couple of recipes for High Tea sandwiches.

When popovers were made at the abbeys, they used a cast iron popover pan. These look similar to a muffin tin, yet they are much deeper. They are readily available at stores that sell cookware.

Ingredients needed to make English Popovers:

1 cup flour   2 eggs, beaten
¾ cup milk   ¼ tsp. salt
¾ cup heavy cream   ⅓ cup ice water

Steps:

1. Preheat the oven to 425°F. Place the popover pan into the oven to heat it. The popover pan must be very hot before you fill it with the batter.

2. In a medium bowl, whisk the flour, milk, cream, eggs, and salt until smooth.

3. Set the bowl aside 5 minutes.

4. Whisk in the ice water until it has fully been incorporated.

5. Spoon the batter evenly into all six popover wells (popover pans have six wells).

6. Place into the oven and bake 45 minutes or until golden brown.

7. Remove from the oven and serve either hot or warm.

Poached Salmon and Cream Cheese Tea Sandwiches

(makes 18)

When it came to the sandwiches of High Tea, there were two types. There was the usual, which was crustless bread cut into festive shapes and spread with a savory cream. Then there was the special, puff pastry cut into rounds and served open-faced. We will center on the festive due to the fact that they are indeed festive. At the abbeys, the puff pastry was made from scratch. For ease and convenience I recommend using the store-bought variety, as making true puff pastry at home can put the home cook into a loony bin!

Though the High Tea sandwiches were indeed dainty, and dainty was usually reserved for the female guests, these sandwiches were offered to both male and female guests. They are all very easy to prepare and an absolute delight to eat.

The savory spread for this sandwich is a luscious poached salmon and cream cheese spread (an abbey favorite) that is lightly hinted with finely minced green onion. You will notice from the picture there is a garnish. High Tea sandwiches were one of the only foods served with a garnish.

Ingredients needed to make Poached Salmon and Cream Cheese Tea Sandwiches:

1 pkg. puff pastry (it contains two sheets, both of which will be used)

½ pound salmon

4 ounces cream cheese, room temperature

1 Tbs. heavy cream

1 green onion, finely minced

¼ tsp. salt

garnish of your choice

Steps:

1. Remove the puff pastry from its box. If frozen, let it thaw. Using a round or decorative cutter, cut the puff pastry into shapes.

2. Preheat the oven to 350°F and line a baking sheet with parchment paper. Place the cut puff pastry pieces onto the prepared baking sheet.

3. In a small sauté pan, bring a few inches of water to a boil. Add the salmon, cover and cook 5 minutes.

4. Remove the salmon from the pan and set aside to cool. Discard the poaching liquid.

5. Place the puff pastry into the oven and bake 15 minutes or until puffed and golden.

6. In a mixer with the paddle attachment, beat the cream cheese, heavy cream, and green onions until smooth.

7. Spoon the cream cheese mixture into a bowl.

8. Using a fork, flake off the salmon meat. Fold the salmon into the cream cheese mixture.

9. Remove the puff pastry from the oven. Remove them from the pan and let them cool on a wire rack.

10. Slice the puff pastries in half lengthwise. Spread the poached salmon and cream cheese mixture on the puff pastry.

11. Garnish the sandwiches and serve.

Cucumber and Cheddar Tea Sandwiches with Horseradish Cream

(makes 18)

It is the most famous of all British sandwiches and was always on the table at High Tea. As a matter of fact, if you travel through Great Britain today and partake in the luxury of High Tea, a cucumber and Cheddar cheese sandwich will be on your plate. It won't be as "classy" as the ones served at the abbey, but it will be tasty nonetheless.

The main difference between an abbey Cucumber and Cheddar Cheese sandwich and the others was in its full-bodied taste. This isn't just a thin slice of cucumber and a piece of cheese. The cooks of the abbeys would never prepare something so simple. This was puff pastry, spread with a horseradish cream, layered with some grated Cheddar cheese, and topped with cucumber and another small dollop of the horseradish cream.

To serve this High Tea sandwich authentically, before you add the thin slice of cucumber you will want to place the cheese-topped puff pastry into the oven to melt the cheese. This is one of the few sandwiches in the culinary world to feature four unique textures in each bite.

Ingredients needed to make Cucumber and Cheddar Cheese Tea Sandwiches:

1 pkg. puff pastry (it contains two sheets, both of which will be used)

¼ cup sour cream

1 Tbs. horseradish

½ tsp. Dijon mustard

½ cup grated Cheddar cheese

1 cucumber, peeled and thinly sliced

Steps:

1. Remove the puff pastry from its box. If frozen, let it thaw. Using a round or decorative cutter, cut the puff pastry into shapes.

2. Preheat the oven to 350°F and line a baking sheet with parchment paper. Place the cut puff pastry pieces onto the prepared baking sheet.

3. Place the puff pastry into the oven and bake 15 minutes or until puffed and golden.

4. Remove the puff pastry from the oven. Remove them from the pan and let cool on a wire rack.

5. In a small bowl, whisk together the sour cream, horseradish, and Dijon mustard until smooth.

6. Slice the puff pastry in half lengthwise and spread each half with some of the horseradish cream, then layer on some of the Cheddar cheese. The cream will hold the cheese in place.

7. Place into the oven and bake a few minutes until the cheese melts.

8. Remove from the oven and top each sandwich with a slice of cucumber.

9. Place the sandwiches on a serving platter, top with a small dollop of the horseradish cream, and serve.

ROASTED SWEET RED PEPPER CREAM TEA SANDWICHES

(makes 18)

During late spring and throughout the summer, the abbeys would host various garden parties and outdoor High Tea. On these occasions the cook was instructed to make the food fresh tasting, meaning to utilize fully the abbey's gardens and homegrown produce. One of the favorite High Tea sandwiches of this time of the year was a very simple, yet very fresh-tasting treat featuring roasted sweet red peppers.

In creating this High Tea sandwich the cook was posed with a problem. The sandwich had to be fresh tasting, yet the cook just couldn't pile onto puff pastry a bevy of sweet peppers. Utilizing common staples of the kitchen, the cook created a cream of subtle taste and rich texture. When the sweet red pepper was added to the cream the fresh taste of the pepper was kept and the cook rewarded with a lovely pastel color.

Due to the fact the sweet pepper growing season was not long throughout Great Britain, when this sandwich was called for other times during the year, the cook would substitute preserved pimentos.

Ingredients needed to make Roasted Sweet Red Pepper Cream Tea Sandwiches:

1 pkg. puff pastry (it contains two sheets, both of which will be used)

4 ounces cream cheese, room temperature

1 Tbs. sour cream

1 Tbs. heavy cream

1 Tbs. minced chives

¼ tsp. salt

½ red bell pepper, roasted, seeded, and minced (this is available in markets)

Steps:

1. Remove the puff pastry from its box. If frozen, let it thaw. Using a round or decorative cutter, cut the puff pastry into shapes.

2. Preheat the oven to 350°F and line a baking sheet with parchment paper. Place the cut puff pastry pieces onto the prepared baking sheet.

3. Place the puff pastry into the oven and bake 15 minutes or until puffed and golden.

4. Remove the puff pastry from the oven. Remove them from the pan and let them cool on a wire rack.

5. In a small bowl, whisk together the cream cheese, sour cream, heavy cream, chives, red pepper, and salt until smooth and spreadable.

6. Slice the puff pastry in half lengthwise and spread each half with some of the roasted sweet pepper cream.

7. Place upon a serving platter, sprinkle with a few chives and serve.

Deviled Salmon and Leek Tea Sandwiches

(makes 18)

As opposed to popular belief, not all of the High Tea sandwiches served were laden with a heavy cream or cream cheese base. This particular High Tea sandwich features neither. It is also one of the richer High Tea sandwiches that was served and one of the tastiest.

Due to the rather robust flavor of this High Tea sandwich it was served mostly to the gentlemen celebrating High Tea. The only time it was noted as being served in a nonsegregated social gathering was when it was presented at a garden party or reception. The leeks and parsnips were a staple of the abbeys as they could be harvested at any time and always be available to the cook from the root cellar. The cooks also used this sandwich as a way to utilize leftover salmon, as this dish can be made with any type of cooked salmon.

Due to the title of this sandwich having the word "deviled" within it, this dish was never served around Christian holidays or celebrations of life (including birthdays).

Ingredients needed to make Deviled Salmon and Leek Tea Sandwiches:

1 pkg. puff pastry (it contains two sheets, both of which will be used)

2 Tbs. olive oil

½ leek, rinsed under cold water and finely chopped

1 parsnip, peeled and julienned (cut into very thin strips)

½ pound cooked salmon, flaked

½ tsp. celery seeds

¼ cup mayonnaise

Cheddar cheese for garnish

Steps:

1. Remove the puff pastry from its box. If frozen, let it thaw. Using a round or decorative cutter, cut the puff pastry into shapes.

2. Preheat the oven to 350°F and line a baking sheet with parchment paper. Place the cut puff pastry pieces onto the prepared baking sheet.

3. Place the puff pastry into the oven and bake 15 minutes or until puffed and golden.

4. Remove the puff pastry from the oven. Remove them from the pan and let them cool on a wire rack.

5. In a medium sauté pan or skillet, heat the olive oil over medium heat. Add the leek and parsnip and sauté 5 minutes.

6. Into the sauté pan, add the salmon and celery seeds. Stir to combine and sauté 3 minutes.

7. Remove the salmon and leek mixture to a medium bowl and fold in the mayonnaise.

8. Slice the puff pastry in half lengthwise and spread each half with some of the deviled salmon and leek.

9. Place the Deviled Salmon and Leek Tea Sandwiches upon a serving platter. Garnish the tops with some Cheddar cheese and serve.

Dinner at the Abbey

❖ ❖ ❖

Breads

ABBEY COUNTRY WHEAT BREAD

(makes 2 loaves)

The protocol of the abbeys was: If you serve a soup, you must serve a bread. Because all dinners at the abbeys consisted of three courses, with one being a soup, bread was a paramount dish. Due to the amount of time to make the breads, it was the first thing the cooks would prepare at the start of their work day.

Abbey Country Wheat Bread was the most common of the breads served. From its subtle crust to the nutty-flavored dough, it went with almost every entrée served. It was presented at the table thinly sliced and slightly warm, thanks to a heated stone (covered by linen) located under the bread tray.

Nothing went to waste at the abbeys. Any leftover bread that was brought back downstairs to the kitchen was either served to the staff or grated into fresh bread crumbs.

Ingredients needed to make Abbey Country Wheat Bread:

2½ cups flour, divided

⅓ cup brown sugar

1 Tbs. yeast

1½ tsp. salt

2 cups warm water

1 Tbs. olive oil

2 cups whole wheat flour

1 egg white

Steps:

1. In a large bowl, stir together 2 cups of flour, and the brown sugar, yeast, salt, and warm water. Set the bowl aside 10 minutes for the yeast to proof (foam).

2. Stir in the olive oil and whole wheat flour until you have a moist dough.

3. Place the dough on a floured surface and knead 10 minutes (this longer kneading time is needed with whole wheat flour).

4. Place the dough back into the bowl, cover with a towel, and let rise 1 hour.

5. Remove the dough from the bowl, place on a floured surface, and knead 5 minutes. Place the dough back into the bowl, cover, and let rise an additional hour.

6. Remove the dough from the bowl and divide in half. Form each half into either a round or elongated loaf.

7. Line a baking sheet with parchment paper or a silicon sheet.

8. Place the formed loaves onto the prepared sheet and let rise 30 minutes.

9. Preheat the oven to 400°F.

10. In a small bowl, whisk the egg white with a little water and brush the loaves with the egg white mixture.

11. Place the bread into the oven and bake 25 minutes.

12. Remove the bread from the oven and place on a wire rack to cool.

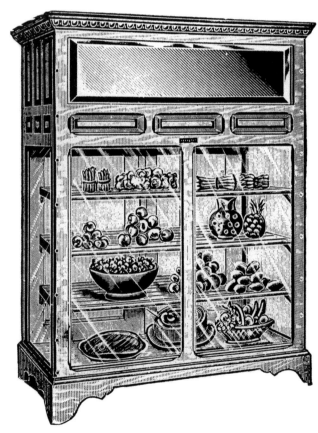

Downton Abbey DINNER BISCUITS

(makes 12 depending on size)

When not entertaining guests the family dinners at Downton Abbey were less formal as far as the food is concerned. For these dinners the bread served was more along the lines of an American biscuit but not just any type of biscuit, a buttery rich flakey biscuit.

Because this particular bread item needed no rising time, they were prepared right along with the dinner in the kitchen and were served at the table piping hot. This type of biscuit was usually the bread dish when the entrée was creamed based or included a gravy. Instead of dipping the biscuit into the cream or the gravy, the family would break off or crumble the biscuit atop it.

This is actually one of the few biscuit recipes in the culinary world that is constructed. After you cut the biscuits with a biscuit cutter (usually round in shape), you will separate the biscuits into pairs. The construction consists of buttering the top of one biscuit and placing another on top. Before going into the oven, you will then butter the top biscuit.

Ingredients needed to make *Downton Abbey* Dinner Biscuits:

4 cups flour

¼ cup sugar

1 Tbs. yeast

1½ tsp. salt

1 cup heavy cream

⅓ cup butter, softened

1 egg

melted butter for brushing

Steps:

1. In a large bowl, whisk together 1½ cups flour, sugar, yeast, and salt until combined. Whisk in the heavy cream and butter until smooth.

2. Into the bowl whisk in the egg and ½ cup flour. Add the remaining flour and stir to form a dough.

3. Place the dough into the refrigerator and chill 30 minutes.

4. Preheat the oven to 375°F. Line a baking sheet with parchment paper or a silicon sheet.

5. Place the dough on a floured surface and roll out to a thickness of ½ inch.

6. Using a round biscuit cutter, cut out 24 biscuits.

7. Divide the biscuits into 12 pairs. Butter the tops of 12 of the biscuits with the melted butter. Place the other biscuit atop and brush that one with melted butter.

8. Place the biscuits on the prepared pan.

9. Place in the oven and bake 20 minutes.

10. Remove the biscuits from the oven and let cool on a wire rack until ready to serve.

ESTATE OAT BREAD

(makes 2 loaves)

The most popular of all English bread is rye bread (and you will find a recipe in this section). The second most popular is one of the variations of their oat bread. This particular oat bread, Estate Oat Bread, was a mainstay at all abbeys. The texture is soft and delicate. The crust is subtly sweet. In a very real way, this is indeed a perfect bread. At the abbeys, they would use steel-cut oats. For today's kitchen I recommend simple rolled oats, but not the "instant" variety.

The preparation of this bread is very different than most. The dough is rather moist and can be quite messy to knead. Instead of implementing any type of the kneading process, if you so desire, you can vigorously stir the dough with a wooden spoon instead and for fans of *Downton Abbey*, you often see the cook, Beryl Patmore, or her assistant Daisy, doing just that. This bread does take some time to prepare as it has three separate rising times.

Whereas most of the loaf varieties of bread served at the abbey dinner table were thinly sliced, this one was not. Due to the consistency of the breads dough, it was thickly sliced and served with entrées consisting of beef, lamb, or pork.

Ingredients needed to make Estate Oat Bread:

2 cups boiling water

2 cups rolled oats (not the "instant" variety)

1 Tbs. butter

2½ tsp. yeast

½ cup warm water

1 Tbs. honey

½ cup brown sugar

4 cups flour, divided

1 tsp. salt

Steps:

1. In a large bowl, stir together the boiling water, rolled oats, and butter. Set the bowl aside 10 minutes to cool.

2. In a small bowl, whisk together the yeast, warm water and honey. Set the bowl aside 5 minutes for the yeast to proof (foam).

3. Once the oat mixture is cool, stir in the proofed yeast.

4. Stir in the brown sugar and 1 cup of flour. Cover the bowl and let the dough rise 1 hour.

5. Stir in the remaining flour and salt. Cover the bowl and let the dough rise 1 hour.

6. Line the bottoms of two 9 × 5 loaf pans with parchment paper.

7. Divide the dough in half and place each half into the prepared pans.

8. Set the pans aside and let the dough rise 1 hour.

9. Preheat the oven to 350°F.

10. Place the breads into the oven and bake 45 minutes.

11. Remove the breads from the oven and let cool in the pan 10 minutes.

12. Remove the breads from their pans to a wire rack and cool until ready to serve.

Sour Cream and Onion Bread

(makes 1 loaf)

This is the only bread served at the abbeys that was eaten with a knife and fork. As a matter-of-fact, at times it was served as one of the courses. There were also rare times when this bread was served during High Tea, where it was presented as thin wedges. It is a delightfully tasty bread with a slight zing thanks to the caramelized onions.

There is no doubt that this is one of the cook's favorite breads, and the reason is simple: As opposed to other breads, it was very quick to make. From the start of preparation to the serving at the table, the elapsed time will be around 45 minutes.

When prepared at an abbey, this bread would be made in a cast iron skillet. Due to the intense heat of the wood-burning ovens, this was the only way to ascertain the rich dough would bake properly and in time with the topping. For today's kitchen, it can be made in a simple round cake pan.

Ingredients needed to make Sour Cream and Onion Bread:

3 Tbs. butter

2 sweet yellow onions, peeled and thinly sliced

2 cups flour

2 tsp. baking powder

1 tsp. salt

¼ cup shortening, chilled

2 Tbs. minced parsley or cilantro

1 cup milk

⅓ cup sour cream

Steps:

1. Preheat the oven to 425°F. Line the bottom of an 8-inch round cake pan with parchment paper.

2. In a medium sauté pan or skillet, melt the butter over medium heat. Add the onions and sauté 10 minutes.

3. In a medium bowl, whisk together the flour, baking powder, and salt. Add the shortening and using a pastry blender or pastry fork, cut the shortening into the flour until it resembles a coarse meal (crumbly).

4. Stir in the parsley and milk until well blended.

5. Spoon the dough into the prepared pan and even out.

6. Spread the caramelized onions over the dough.

7. Spread the sour cream over the onions.

8. Place into the oven and bake 25 minutes.

9. Remove from the oven and let cool in the pan 10 minutes.

10. Remove from the pan, cut into wedges, and serve.

Downton Dinner Rolls

(makes 12 rolls)

During many of the episodes of *Downton Abbey* you see the downstairs staff sitting around their meal table. In many of these scenes you see bowls of soup or stew in front of them and somewhere on the table you see little round loaves of bread. Those loaves are Downton Dinner Rolls. These rolls have a nice, dark, crunchy crust, a light dough, and a wonderful hint of sweetness.

These dinner rolls would only be served in the upstairs dining room during family meals. If there were guests or dignitaries, they would not be served as it was considered rude to have a guest cut or tear his or her own bread.

Not only is this a very simple dinner roll to prepare, it is also one of the tastiest. Whereas most breads of this type can be quite boring on their own, the sweetness of this bread makes it a perfect accompaniment for any entrée with a beef-based sauce or gravy.

Ingredients needed to make Downton Dinner Rolls:

3½ cups flour

¼ cup sugar

2 tsp. salt

2½ tsp. yeast

1¾ cups water

Steps:

1. In a large bowl, combine all the ingredients and stir with a wooden spoon to form a dough.

2. Place the dough on a floured surface and knead 10 minutes.

3. Place the dough back into the bowl, cover, and let rise 1 hour.

4. Without removing the dough, punch it down (yes, put your fist into it). Cover the bowl again and let it rise one more hour.

5. Remove the dough to a floured surface and divide the dough into 12 pieces.

6. Flatten each piece of dough into a disc of ½-inch thickness.

7. Line a baking sheet with parchment paper or a silicon sheet.

8. Place the rolls on the prepared baking sheet and let rise 30 minutes.

9. Preheat the oven to 450°F.

10. Place into the oven and bake 20 minutes.

11. Remove from the oven and place the rolls on a wire rack to cool.

Cottage Cheese Bread

(makes 12 depending on size)

Cheese was an important food staple at the abbeys. It was incorporated into many dishes and because most of the cheeses used were actually made at the abbey, it was very economic as well. Cottage Cheese Bread, or as it was also known, Curd Cheese Bread, was the most popular bread to be served with any entrée that featured seafood.

In today's terms, this bread would be considered a biscuit, yet probably unlike any biscuit you have tried before. The use of cottage cheese in the dough gives this bread a wondrous texture and a lighter-than-usual exterior. The bread gets its golden hue due to the fact it is brushed with a beaten egg yolk before it enters the oven.

Because there is essentially no liquid used in the preparation of Cottage Cheese Bread, it has a very short shelf life. It must be eaten the day it is baked. At the abbey, if there was any leftover, it would be sent downstairs to the staff to be enjoyed during their last meal of the day.

Ingredients needed to make Cottage Cheese Bread:

2 cups flour

¾ tsp. salt

1 cup butter, chilled and diced

1 cup small curd cottage cheese

1 egg yolk, beaten

Steps:

1. In a medium bowl, whisk the flour and salt. Add the butter and using a pastry blender or a pastry fork, cut the butter into the flour until it resembles a coarse meal (crumbly).

2. Stir the cottage cheese into the flour mixture until you have a dough.

3. Remove the dough to a floured surface and knead 5 minutes.

4. Roll the dough into a rectangle and then fold it into thirds.

5. Repeat step 4 and then wrap the dough in plastic wrap and chill 1 hour.

6. Preheat the oven to 400°F. Line a baking sheet with parchment paper or a silicon sheet.

7. Unwrap the dough and place it upon a floured surface. Roll the dough out to a thickness of ¼-inch.

8. Using a round biscuit cutter, cut out the biscuits.

9. Place the biscuits onto the prepared baking sheet and brush the tops with the beaten egg yolk.

10. Place into the oven and bake 10 minutes.

11. Remove from the oven and place on a wire rack to cool.

Yorkshire Rye Bread

(makes 2 loaves)

Aside from the typical white bread, there is probably no "soft" bread more popular in the world than rye bread—and there is no country in the world that has more types of rye bread than England. During the Victorian and Edwardian eras throughout Great Britain, each abbey had its own version as each cook put his or her own special touch to each loaf.

Yorkshire Rye Bread would have been the perfect rye bread for Downton Abbey, as its personality greatly matches the Downton cook, Beryl Patmore, a little sweet and very crusty. This bread was one of only a few dishes prepared at the abbeys that if there was any leftover it would be served again to the family. In most cases, leftovers were sent downstairs to the staff. In the case of this bread, however, if there was any leftover, the following day it would be toasted and served for breakfast with sweet creamery butter and orange marmalade.

Yorkshire Rye Bread is also a wonderful bread to use for High Tea. Just slice the rye bread thinly, remove the crust, and cut into festive shapes before layering it with a savory spread.

Ingredients needed to make Yorkshire Rye Bread:

2½ cups flour, divided

⅓ cup brown sugar

1 Tbs. yeast

1 Tbs. caraway seeds

1½ tsp. salt

2 cups warm water

1 Tbs. corn oil

2 cups rye flour

1 egg white

1 Tbs. cold water

Steps:

1. In a large bowl whisk together the 2 cups of flour, brown sugar, yeast, caraway seeds, and salt. Stir in the warm water and oil until well combined. Set the bowl aside 10 minutes.

2. Stir ½ cup of flour into the bowl to form a soft dough. Stir in the rye flour to form a stiff dough.

3. Place the dough on a floured surface and knead 10 minutes.

4. Place the dough back into the bowl, cover, and let rise 1 hour.

5. Remove the dough from the bowl and divide in half. Form each half into a round loaf.

6. Line a baking sheet with parchment paper or a silicon sheet.

7. Place the breads on the prepared baking sheet and let rise 1 hour.

8. Preheat the oven to 400°F.

9. In a small bowl, whisk the egg white and cold water.

10. Brush the loaves with the egg white mixture.

11. Place the breads into the oven and bake 35 minutes.

12. Remove the breads from the oven and let cool on a wire rack.

Soups

Royal Cheddar Cheese Soup

(serves 4)

At the abbeys, during the Edwardian era it was protocol that if you served bread with a meal, you must serve soup. During this era the most popular soup among the aristocrats was the satiny smooth splendor of Royal Cheddar Cheese Soup. There may not be a more quintessential English soup as it contains many of the elements of English cooking, including potatoes, onions, cream, and cheese.

Royal Cheddar Cheese Soup was always served at dinners when special guests were present. If you watch the television show *Downton Abbey*, you have noticed that the footman in the dining room always presents the food to the guests and the guests put whatever amount of food they would like upon their plate. With soups, this was a little different. With soups, the footman would ladle the soup into a shallow bowl and present the bowl to the guest.

It is also interesting to note that the soups of the abbey were never served hot. They were always served at a temperature where the guest would not have to blow on the soup before eating it as blowing on a spoon of soup was considered uncouth.

Ingredients needed to make Royal Cheddar Cheese Soup:

1 Tbs. butter

2 yellow onions, peeled and chopped

2 potatoes, peeled and cubed

4 cloves garlic, peeled and minced

6 cups chicken stock

½ tsp. dry mustard

1 cup heavy cream

2 cups grated sharp Cheddar cheese

½ tsp. hot pepper sauce

3 Tbs. minced chives

Steps:

1. In a medium saucepan, melt the butter over medium heat. Add the onions, potatoes, and garlic and sauté 10 minutes.

2. Add the chicken stock and bring to a boil. Reduce the heat to simmer and cook 10 minutes.

3. Remove the contents of the saucepan to a food processor and puree.

4. In the saucepan, over medium heat, whisk together the dry mustard and heavy cream.

5. Stir the puree into the saucepan and simmer 5 minutes.

6. Stir in the Cheddar cheese and hot sauce and keep stirring until the cheese has melted.

7. Ladle into serving bowls, top with some chives, and serve.

Cabbage and Rice Soup

(serves 4)

There are a few things you might notice from the soups included in this book. First, all of them are rather hearty. Second, most of the ingredients were all grown or produced at the abbey. Third, they are all rather quick to prepare. None of this is by accident!

Cabbage and Rice Soup was a seasonal soup at the abbeys. It was considered winter fare. The cabbage, onions, and carrots used for the soup would be harvested the day the soup was to be made for the ultimate in flavor. It is interesting to note that the cook would always remove the core of the cabbage before preparation. The reason being that the core of the cabbage, when cooked, creates an unpleasant aroma. The cook would often save the cores and use them to make a slaw for the staff or pickle them for a later use.

This recipe calls for brown rice, yet if the head housekeeper could not find brown rice (the head housekeeper was in charge of procuring food for the kitchen), the soup would be prepared using diced potatoes, or if a creamy texture was requested by the lady of the house, leftover mashed potatoes would be used.

Ingredients needed to make Cabbage and Rice Soup:

3 Tbs. butter

1 head cabbage, core removed and shredded

1 yellow onion, peeled and chopped

2 carrots, peeled and chopped

8 cups chicken stock

2 Tbs. minced dill

1 cup brown rice

1 tsp. salt

1 tsp. ground black pepper

Steps:

1. In a large sauté pan, melt the butter over medium heat. Add the cabbage, onion, and carrots and sauté 10 minutes.

2. Stir in the chicken stock and dill and bring to a boil. Reduce the heat to simmer and cook 15 minutes.

3. Stir in the rice, salt, and black pepper and cook 25 minutes before serving.

Potato and Pea Soup

(serves 4)

This is one of the few soups prepared at the abbey that uses beef stock as base. Though the abbeys raised most of their own animals for food, cows were seldom raised due to the amount of land needed to graze them. As you will notice in the "Entrées" section of this book, beef was not often prepared at the abbeys, nor was it very popular during the Edwardian era.

What separates this soup from the other soups of this genre is the texture. Whereas most of the potato or pea soups of this era were creamed, the cooks of the abbeys centered on the palate of the guests. Each spoonful was to represent the freshness of the ingredients and the gardens of the abbey. There was the sweetness of the peas, the savory of the onions, and the tenderness of the potatoes.

For today's cook, it is rather difficult to find fresh peas at the market. If you cannot find them, you can use the flash-frozen variety (they retain their natural sweetness) with no alteration to the recipe.

Ingredients needed to make Potato and Pea Soup:

2 Tbs. butter

2 Tbs. corn oil

2 yellow onions, peeled and thinly sliced

1 tsp. salt

2 cloves garlic, minced

3 cups diced potatoes

4 cups beef stock

2 cups peas

1 tsp. ground black pepper

Steps:

1. In a medium saucepan, melt the butter in the oil over medium heat. Add the onions and salt and sauté 10 minutes.

2. Stir in the garlic, potatoes, and beef stock and bring to a boil. Reduce the heat to a simmer, cover, and cook 30 minutes.

3. Add the peas and black pepper and cook 10 minutes before serving.

PEARL BARLEY SOUP

(serves 4)

Thick, rich, creamy, and bursting with flavor is the best way to describe this abbey classic. One of the more versatile soups of the era, it was served year-round and was often the featured soup at all garden parties and festivities.

The luxurious and satiny smooth thickness of this soup is created by the combination of the egg yolks and heavy cream. This is indeed a very rich soup and was served in smaller quantities than most of the other soups. When this soup was served for an engagement or wedding party, the cook would often substitute parsnips for carrots to give it a more white or virginal presentation.

The ham used for this dish would come directly from the smokehouses located on the abbey grounds. For today's cook, you can use any type of cured ham available or even bacon.

Ingredients needed to make Pearl Barley Soup:

2 Tbs. butter

1 yellow onion, peeled and chopped

1 leek, tender white part only, chopped

2 carrots, peeled and chopped

2 stalks celery, chopped

½ cup smoked ham, julienned

½ cup pearl barley

1 Tbs. flour

4 cups chicken stock

2 egg yolks, beaten

⅓ cup heavy cream

Steps:

1. In a medium sauté pan, melt the butter over medium heat. Add the onion, leek, carrots, and celery and sauté 5 minutes. Add the ham and barley and cook 2 minutes.

2. In a medium bowl, whisk together the flour and the chicken stock.

3. Stir the chicken stock into the sauté pan and bring to a boil. Reduce the heat to a simmer and cook 90 minutes (the barley will expand).

4. In a small bowl, whisk together the yolks and the cream.

5. Slowly add the yolks to the soup while you stir. Cook the soup 6 minutes and then serve.

ENGLISH CREAMED CHICKEN SOUP

(serves 4)

Creamed Chicken Soup was one of the more popular soups of the Edwardian era throughout Great Britain. Away from the abbeys, this soup was a way to use leftover chicken and was rather bland. At the abbeys, the chicken was prepared specifically for this soup and when served, was nothing but the chicken and the very rich cream.

In preparing the chicken, the cooks did something rather interesting: Before cooking the whole chicken, they would pound it with a mallet or a rolling pin. In doing this, they broke the bones of the chicken, which resulted in more taste in the stock. To enhance the taste of the soup even more, they made their stock with less water than usual, which of course meant a less-diluted flavor.

When you read this recipe, you will notice that the chicken bones, skin, and the vegetables are discarded after they are cooked. In an abbey kitchen, this would not be the case. In the abbey kitchen, the cook would add these to some simmering water and make a weaker chicken stock to use for soups prepared for the staff.

Ingredients needed to make Creamed Chicken Soup:

1 whole chicken, innards removed

6 cups water

2 stalks celery, chopped

1 bay leaf

1 onion, unpeeled and quartered

1 tsp. salt

4 whole black peppercorns

3 Tbs. flour

1 cup heavy cream, divided

1 cup milk

3 Tbs. butter

Steps:

1. In a large stockpot over high heat, add the chicken, water, celery, bay leaf, onion, salt, and peppercorns. Bring to a boil. Reduce the heat to a simmer, cover, and cook 2 hours.

2. Remove the chicken from the pot and set aside to cool.

3. Strain the cooking liquid through a fine sieve and discard any solids. Pour the stock back into the pot.

4. Remove the meat from the chicken and discard any bones, skin, and fat.

5. In a small bowl, whisk the flour and ½ cup of the heavy cream until the flour has dissolved. Whisk this mixture into the stock.

6. Whisk the remaining cream, milk, and butter into the soup and bring to a boil.

7. Reduce the heat to simmer. Add the chicken and cook 5 minutes before serving.

Majestic Potato Cream

(serves 4)

There are potato soups and there are potato soups, but there is no potato soups as rich and elegant as Majestic Potato Cream, a very thick potato soup with a subtle hint of spice and fit for royalty. As a matter-of-fact, this soups was only prepared if a member of King Edward's staff was present for a dinner or gala.

As opposed to other soups, which were served in shallow bowls, this soup was served in a little cup that resembled a typical custard cup or a saucer-type plate with a slight indentation in the middle. The reason for the smaller than normal serving was the intense richness of the soup. To add even more richness and creamy texture to the soup, the cook would often use triple cream instead of heavy cream.

Though this soup might be a little rich for today's palate, it can be made by substituting the heavy cream with half-and-half. If you were to use only milk you would lose considerable texture and taste.

Ingredients needed to make Majestic Potato Cream:

2 cups mashed potatoes

2 cups milk

1 cup heavy cream

½ tsp. salt

¼ tsp. ground white pepper

¼ tsp. ground allspice

¼ cup butter

paprika for sprinkling

Steps:

1. In a medium saucepan over medium heat, whisk all the ingredients, except the butter, and bring to a boil.

2. Reduce the heat to simmer and cook 5 minutes.

3. Ladle the soup into serving bowls, top with a pat of butter, sprinkle with paprika, and serve.

Stilton Chowder

(serves 4)

There is not a more authentic English soup in the world than Stilton Chowder. Stilton cheese was created in the village of Stilton, England, in 1730 and to this date, by law, a cheese cannot carry the title "Stilton" unless it was produced in either Derbyshire, Leicestershire, or Nottinghamshire. Outside of England, this soup is often made with bleu cheese as often times bleu cheese is confused with Stilton cheese due to its close visual resemblance.

This very special soup was prepared only by the cook of the abbey and never by an assistant for the simple reason that if the soup goes even one degree over a simmer, it is ruined. An intense heat breaks down the cheese and the regal creaminess of the soup cannot be achieved.

This soup has more savory ingredients than other cheese-based soups due to the strong aroma and taste of Stilton cheese. The savory ingredients aid in tempering the intensity of the cheese. The serving of this soup was always accompanied by a rye bread and at Downton Abbey that rye bread would be Yorkshire Rye Bread (recipe included in this section).

Ingredients needed to make Stilton Chowder:

¼ cup butter	¼ cup flour
1 yellow onion, chopped	3 cups chicken stock
1 carrot, peeled and chopped	2 cups milk
1 stalk celery, chopped	½ pound Stilton cheese, crumbled
1 bay leaf	1 tsp. Dijon mustard

Steps:

1. In a medium saucepan, melt the butter over medium heat. Add the onion, carrot, celery, and bay leaf and sauté 5 minutes.

2. Stir in the flour until well combined.

3. Stir in the stock and milk until smooth and thickened.

4. Stir in the cheese and mustard and continue stirring until the cheese has melted and the soup is smooth.

5. Bring soup just to the point of a simmer. Do not let it come to a boil.

6. Ladle the soup into bowls and serve.

Side Dishes

Abbey Baked Eggs and Mushrooms in Cheddar Cream

(serves 4)

This is actually quite an elegant dish for ingredients so simple, but such were the talents of the cooks of the abbeys. It is very quick to prepare, so it reaches the table hot, and laden with the freshness of abbey-grown and produced goods. When the mushrooms were brought into the kitchen by a member of the abbey gardening staff, they were handed off to the scullery maid who would take each mushroom and with a damp lint-free cloth wipe it to remove the dirt. The stems of the mushrooms would be removed (and used for a mushroom soup for the staff), and the caps sent off to the cook.

Even though this dish does have some accents of French cooking, which was beginning to become popular in England during the Edwardian era, it is indeed quite British. A very popular side dish to serve with any entrée consisting of seafood, it also made its way to the tables of spring and summer abbey garden parties.

Authentically, these were prepared in round pans with no handles and then transferred to platters for presentation at the table. For today's kitchen, it would be much easier to prepare them in ovenproof au gratin dishes, which are rather inexpensive and can be found in most kitchenware stores.

Ingredients needed to make Abbey Baked Eggs and Mushrooms in Cheddar Cream:

2 Tbs. butter

2 cups sliced mushrooms

2 green onions, minced

1 tsp. minced thyme

4 eggs

¼ cup heavy cream

½ cup grated Cheddar cheese

Steps:

1. Preheat the oven to 350°F and lightly brush four small au gratin dishes with oil.

2. In a medium sauté pan, melt the butter over medium heat. Add the mushrooms, green onions, and thyme and sauté 5 minutes.

3. Divide the mushroom mixture among the prepared au gratin dishes.

4. Make a small well (opening) in the mushroom mixture and carefully add the egg (you don't want the yolk to break).

5. Drizzle some cream around the egg and then sprinkle some of the Cheddar cheese over the dish.

6. Place into the oven and bake 10 minutes.

7. Remove from the oven and let cool slightly before serving.

ASPARAGUS IN CIDER SAUCE

(serves 4)

If you were to venture back in time and take a stroll through the gardens of the abbeys, your eyes would take in the marvelous sight of wild asparagus wherever it could find a plot of earth to take root. During the short growing season in England, these slim and tender spears would make their way to the kitchen daily, and at night, would be the star taste in some wonderful side dishes.

Asparagus in Cider Sauce was a favorite side dish for any entrée featuring seafood, as the acidity of the cider sauce greatly enhanced the flavor of the seafood. The spears of asparagus used for all of these dishes were of a tender variety, as the spears were prepared whole, and it was preferred to cut through them with a fork and not a knife.

For today's kitchen, to get the full taste and tenderness of this dish, because wild asparagus is not found in markets, you will want to peel the asparagus. Starting from the bud end (tip), peel down until you reach the vibrant green part of the stem and then cut off the woodsy white bottom part.

Ingredients needed to make Asparagus in Cider Sauce:

1 pound asparagus, trimmed if necessary
1 Tbs. butter
2 tsp. flour
1 tsp. salt
¼ tsp. ground black pepper

⅛ tsp. ground nutmeg
⅓ cup cider vinegar
⅔ cup heavy cream
¼ tsp. lemon juice

Steps:

1. In a large sauté pan, bring a few inches of water to a boil. Add the asparagus and cook 10 minutes or until tender, depending on the size. Drain the asparagus and set it aside. Discard the cooking liquid.

2. In a small saucepan, melt the butter over medium heat. Stir in the flour, salt, black pepper, and nutmeg until well combined. This is what is referred to as a seasoned roux (thickener).

3. Whisk the cider vinegar and whipping cream into the saucepen and whisk until the sauce begins to simmer. Reduce the heat to low and cook 5 minutes.

4. Stir in the lemon juice.

5. Place the asparagus on a serving platter.

6. Drape the sauce over the asparagus and serve.

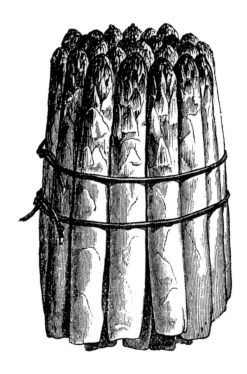

Port Sautéed Baby Mushrooms

(serves 4)

As anyone even vaguely knowledgeable of England knows, it can be quite a damp country most of the year and this makes it perfect for growing mushrooms. All of the abbeys grew a wonderful variety mushrooms in many types and sizes, and they were used in many dishes from High Tea to a regal dinner.

The proper mushrooms for this dish are the smaller varieties. If you buy your mushrooms at the market, you would want the button mushrooms. The mushrooms should be small so they can easily fit on the fork with a piece of meat and be quickly sautéed to perfection.

The use of alcohol in food preparation was very rare in the abbeys. This is one of the very few dishes that includes alcohol even though alcohol and wine were readily available to members of the family and invited guests.

Port Sautéed Baby Mushrooms would be the side dish for an entrée featuring beef or lamb, and was always the side dish at large galas that featured large roasts, which were carved at the table.

Ingredients needed to make Port Sautéed Baby Mushrooms:

1 pound small mushrooms, stems removed

¼ cup olive oil

2 Tbs. butter

2 shallots, minced

¼ cup port

Steps:

1. If the mushrooms are store bought, wipe them with a damp cloth to remove any soil. Do not wash them.

2. In a medium sauté pan, melt the butter into the olive oil over medium heat. Add the shallots and sauté 2 minutes.

3. Add the mushrooms and sauté 5 minutes.

4. Carefully pour in the port and cook 5 minutes before serving.

Baked Cream Turnips

(serves 4)

In various episodes on *Downton Abbey,* when the scene moves into the dining room you will see the footman offering a dish that resembles mashed potatoes, yet the guests use a spatula to remove it to their plate. What they are actually being served is Baked Cream Turnips, which means the entrée is a dish featuring fowl, as root vegetables were the common side dish for such entrées.

Variations of this dish are quite common in the American South, where turnips are quite popular. This English version differs due to its richness and the bread crumbs they use to top it, which gives the turnips a slight crunch. Because turnips can be an acquired taste, this dish can also be prepared quite nicely by using parsnips.

Because the abbeys grew their own produce, you might be wondering what they did with the turnip greens (the stem and leaves), which are a popular dish in many parts of the world. There are two possibilities: They either used them for staff meals or fed them to the livestock, as there are no dishes from this era served at the abbeys that utilized them.

Ingredients needed to make Baked Cream Turnips:

2 pounds turnips, greens removed, peeled and diced

2 Tbs. butter

2 Tbs. heavy cream

1 tsp. salt

½ tsp. ground white pepper

¼ tsp. ground nutmeg

1 cup fresh bread crumbs

3 Tbs. olive oil

Steps:

1. Preheat the oven to 350°F.

2. Into a large saucepan of boiling water, add the turnips and cook 10 minutes or until fork tender. Drain the turnips and discard the water.

3. Place the turnips into a food processor and puree. Spoon the puree into a medium bowl.

4. Stir into the turnips the butter, heavy cream, salt, pepper, and nutmeg.

5. Spoon the turnip mixture into an ovenproof baking dish. Layer the bread crumbs over the turnips and drizzle with the olive oil.

6. Place into the oven and bake 40 minutes before serving.

Potato and Smoked Ham Soufflé

(serves 4)

There is a rather amusing scene in season one of *Downton Abbey* centering around a soufflé. Mrs. Patmore, the abbey cook, just takes a soufflé out of the oven. As the footmen are carrying the food toward the dining room, she realizes they have forgotten the soufflé. She hands the soufflé to one of the maids and in a frenzy yells at her, "Hurry up and get it to them before it falls!" Such is the bane of making a soufflé.

Actually a soufflé is very easy to make, and this soufflé, along with the cheese soufflé, were the most popular at the abbeys and served quite often with any entrée. A typical potato soufflé, though pleasant to look at, can be quite boring to eat. That is not the case with this potato soufflé, as it is dotted throughout with chopped smoked ham. If there was no smoked ham available at the abbey when the cook was preparing this dish, he/she would use smoked bacon.

When preparing this soufflé, you want to remember the words of Mrs. Patmore and get it to the table before it falls. From the time it leaves the oven to the time it begins to deflate (fall) you have about 10 minutes.

Ingredients needed to make Potato and Smoked Ham Soufflé:

1½ pounds potatoes, peeled and diced

¼ cup butter

⅔ cup heavy cream

4 eggs, separated

½ cup minced smoked ham

½ tsp. ground white pepper

Steps:

1. Preheat the oven to 375°F.

2. Into a large pot of boiling water, add the potatoes and cook 10 minutes or until fork tender.

3. Place the potatoes into a food processor and puree. Spoon the puree into a large bowl.

4. Stir in the butter and heavy cream.

5. Stir in the egg yolks, one at a time, until well blended and then stir in the smoked ham.

6. In a mixer with the whisk attachment, beat the egg white until stiff peaks form. Fold the egg white into the potatoes.

7. Spoon the mixture into a 2-quart soufflé dish (do not oil the soufflé dish or it won't rise high) and sprinkle the top with the ground white pepper.

8. Place into the oven and bake 45 minutes. Do not open the oven door to check it!

9. Remove from the oven and serve within 10 minutes.

Baked Brussels Sprouts and Cheddar Cheese

(serves 4)

If you go through any English cookbook, whether it be a classic or something modern from the great Chef Jamie Oliver, and you are bound to find recipes featuring Brussels sprouts. There are even family crests featuring what many people mistakenly call mini cabbages. These incredible healthy vegetables are as associated with England as is Cheddar cheese, and with this dish you get to enjoy both.

Cheddar cheese has been an aristocratic food staple since 1170, when King Henry II decided that because he liked it then all his subjects should like it as well, and he would order immense amounts of it from the village of Cheddar in Somerset county. Due to its creamy texture when melted, it became a mainstay in many dishes, and due to its rather inexpensive cost, it could be enjoyed by all the classes or people.

If you're hesitant to try this dish because you don't like Brussels sprouts, you could do two things. First, remove the core from the sprouts before cooking and you won't get that sulfuric smell, which is the main reason people don't like them. Secondly, make the dish with cauliflower, which was another way it was presented at the abbeys.

Ingredients needed to make Baked Brussels Sprouts and Cheddar Cheese:

1½ pounds Brussels sprouts

½ tsp. salt

1 Tbs. butter

1½ cups grated Cheddar cheese

1 tsp. ground black pepper

Steps:

1. Preheat the oven to 325°F.

2. Slice each Brussels sprout in half and remove the core and any discolored leaves.

3. In a medium sauté pan, bring 1 inch of water to a boil. Add the sprouts and salt and cook 3 minutes.

4. With a slotted spoon remove the sprouts and place them into an ovenproof baking dish. Add the butter to the sprouts and toss to coat them.

5. Layer the cheese and black pepper over the sprouts and cover the dish with foil.

6. Place into the oven and bake 20 minutes.

7. Remove from the oven and let cool 5 minutes before serving.

Savory Caraway Cabbage

(serves 4)

Cabbage grew year-round in the abbey gardens and was used for everything from entrées to side dishes to being stuffed and featured at High Tea. If you were to walk into the root cellar of the abbey, you would also see at least one large barrel where sauerkraut was being cured. The only thing it really wasn't being used for was one of its most famous dishes, coleslaw, as there are no records of this salad ever being served at an English abbey.

There is an amusing story about this dish. As I was talking to a chef from Devonshire, I asked him how this dish came about. He shrugged his shoulders and said, "The cook was probably making rye bread and the bowl of caraway seeds fell into the cabbage." This very well may be true, as before the Edwardian era I could find no dish similar to this. If it was an accident then it was a tasty one, as caraway seeds and cabbage create a wonderful marriage of taste.

Because the cabbage will be cooked for a while, you will want to make sure to remove its core. It can produce an sulfuric aroma and taint the natural subtle sweetness of the cabbage.

Ingredients needed to make Savory Caraway Cabbage:

¼ cup butter

1 head cabbage, core removed and leaves shredded

1 onion, peeled and thinly sliced

½ cup water

3 tomatoes, chopped

1 tsp. salt

1½ Tbs. caraway seeds

2 Tbs. sugar

Steps:

1. In a medium sauté pan, melt the butter over medium heat. Add the cabbage and onion and sauté 10 minutes.

2. Add the remaining ingredients and stir to combine.

3. Place a cover on the pan and cook 30 minutes before serving.

Asparagus with Egg, Garlic, and Lemon Juice

(serves 4)

This is one of the most regal of all British asparagus dishes and was usually reserved to being served only on special occasions. As you might have noticed from the recipes in this book, garlic was used sparingly at the abbeys. The reason for this is the breath of the guests. In this dish, the lemon tempers the taste of the garlic thus rendering the breath of the guests more fresh for those close conversations.

There are actually two ways to prepare this dish. You can prepare it as the recipe dictates or in place of a hardboiled egg, you can use a pickled egg. When this dish was prepared for King Edward at one of his palaces, the cook would use whole quail eggs.

Due to the ingredients and various tastes of this dish, it is a wonderful side dish for any entrée and will greatly accentuate all roasted type of meats.

Ingredients needed to make Asparagus with Egg, Garlic, and Lemon Juice:

5 Tbs. butter

3 cloves garlic, peeled and minced

2 pounds asparagus, white lower ends removed

3 Tbs. lemon juice

1 hardboiled egg, shelled and chopped

2 tsp. minced tarragon

Steps:

1. In a small sauté pan, melt the butter over medium heat. Add the garlic and sauté 1 minute. Remove the pan from the heat and set aside.

2. Place the asparagus into a large pot of boiling water and cook 5 minutes or until tender (depends on size of spears). Drain the asparagus and discard the water.

3. Into the sautéed garlic, stir the lemon juice and egg.

4. Place the asparagus on a serving platter and spoon the garlic and egg mixture atop.

5. Sprinkle the dish with tarragon and serve.

Shredded Spiced Brussels Sprouts

(serves 4)

There has always been a misconception about English food being dull and boring and lacking any spice. I think—and hope—the recipes in this book will put the myth of dull and boring to rest. As far as the spiciness goes, this dish does have some slight heat. From all accounts, this dish was only served around the winter holidays, and the reason for that might be the fact the included cayenne pepper can warm one rather quickly.

This dish is pure freshness. The Brussels sprouts are blanched (quickly cooked in water) and their incredible taste, slightly sweet and nutty, is the focus. Don't worry about the cayenne pepper, as the lemon juice will temper the spiciness. The butter adds the perfect amount of richness and regal gleam to the finished dish.

An interesting side note to this dish: If there were any leftovers brought back to the kitchen, the next morning the abbey cook would mix it with some scrambled eggs for the staff's morning meal.

Ingredients needed for Shredded Spiced Brussels Sprouts:

4 cups Brussels sprouts

½ cup butter

2 tsp. lemon juice

1 tsp. salt

½ tsp. ground white pepper

½ tsp. cayenne peppers

Steps:

1. Using a sharp paring knife, cut out the core of the Brussels sprouts and remove any discolored leaves. Shred the Brussels sprouts by thinly slicing them in any direction.

2. In a medium saucepan of boiling water, place the sprouts and cook them 5 minutes. Drain the sprouts and discard the water.

3. Place the sprouts into a serving bowl. Add the remaining ingredients, toss to coat, and serve.

Entrées

EDWARDIAN LEG OF LAMB

(serves 4)

According to lore, one of the cooks for King Edward created this recipe for a special Christmas gathering of guests at the palace. It was received so well that it soon became a staple for special occasions at all the abbeys throughout Great Britain. For this dish, every ingredient used was grown or produced on the grounds of the abbey, with the sole exception of the sugar. Once you prepare this dish you will come to the full realization why it became so popular.

Lamb was a very popular dish in England during the Edwardian era. The abbeys took great pride in their sheep herds and these herds would often feed the entire township or county where the abbey was located. There are three degrees of lamb and all were used for food consumption: lamb (under one year old); hogget (one to two years old); and mutton (adult).

Any type of apple can be used to prepare this dish. At the abbeys, they used a sweet red variety from their orchards. Today when this dish is served, the chef will often use a more tart apple, such as a Granny Smith, to compliment the taste of the lamb and spices.

Ingredients needed to make Edwardian Leg of Lamb:

1 5-pound leg of lamb, trimmed of excess fat

1 Tbs. minced thyme

1 Tbs. minced marjoram

1 Tbs. minced sage

8 garlic cloves, peeled and whole

⅓ cup sugar

⅓ cup cider vinegar

3 Tbs. water

3 Tbs. honey

2 cinnamon sticks

½ tsp. ground cloves

½ tsp. minced ginger

3 apples, peeled, cored and cut into 8 wedges

Steps:

1. Preheat the oven to 325°F.

2. Place the leg of lamb on a roasting rack within a roasting pan. Rub the lamb with the thyme, marjoram, and sage.

3. Using a sharp paring knife, make deep slits into the lamb and plug each slit with a clove of garlic.

4. Place the lamb into the oven and roast 2½ hours.

5. Remove the lamb from the oven and cover with a foil tent to keep warm. Do not turn off the oven.

6. In a large sauté pan over medium heat, combine the sugar, vinegar, water, honey, cinnamon sticks, cloves, and ginger and bring to a boil.

7. Add the apples to the pan. Lower the heat to simmer and cook the apples 7 minutes.

8. With a sharp paring life, make deep slits all over the lamb and plug each with a apple wedge. Spoon the apple cooking sauce over the lamb.

9. Remove the foil from the lamb and place it back into the oven to roast for 20 minutes.

10. Remove the lamb from the oven and let rest on a carving board 10 minutes.

11. Carve the lamb and place on a serving platter with the apples.

Cider House Hens

(serves 4)

Most of the abbeys of Great Britain during the late Victorian and the Edwardian eras had cider houses on the property. Because the fictionalized Downton Abbey was in Yorkshire, the chances are very strong it would have had a cider house and this incredible dish would have been one of the star dinner entrées. A cider house was where the apples grown at the abbey were stored and made into various ciders, both hard (fermented for alcohol) and soft (nonalcoholic). This dish can be made with either variety, albeit the soft variety would have been chosen for dinners where dignitaries were guests.

This dish has been adapted for today's kitchen because at the abbeys they would have used guinea hens instead of Cornish game hens. The usual style of presentation for this would be a half of a hen served to each guest. For the female dinner guests, the footmen might (not always) cut the hen into serving pieces just before presentation.

In our research of this dish, we could find no particular type of apple which was used. The recipes we found simply said "apples." Chef Larry Edwards has chosen green apples for this dish (Granny Smith) as the tartness will greatly accentuated the tastes of both the hens and the bacon.

Ingredients needed to make Cider House Hens:

2 Cornish game hens, split in half
   salt and black pepper to taste
¼ cup vegetable oil
4 slices smoked bacon, chopped
1¼ cups apple cider (not apple juice)
⅓ cup brandy

1 cup heavy cream
2 green apples, peeled, cored, and sliced
2 Tbs. butter
1 Tbs. sugar
1 lemon, juice only
½ cup walnuts, chopped

Steps:

1. Preheat the oven to 400°F.

2. Wipe the hens of any excess moisture, both inside and out. Season the hens with salt and pepper

3. In a large sauté pan, heat the oil over medium heat. Add the hens and brown on both sides.

4. Remove the hens to a platter.

5. Add the bacon to the sauté pan and sauté 3 minutes.

6. Remove the pan from the heat and add the apple cider and brandy (never add liquor to a pan while on the heat). Place the pan back onto the heat and bring to a boil. Reduce the heat to a simmer and cook until it has been reduced by one-third.

7. Stir in the cream until well incorporated. Place the hens into the pan.

8. Place a lid on the pan, place into the oven, and cook 45 minutes.

9. In a medium sauté pan, melt the butter over medium heat.

10. Add the apples and sugar and sauté the apples about 5 minutes per side.

11. Remove the hens from the oven and place on a serving platter. Add the apples around the hens.

12. Just before serving, squeeze the lemon juice over the dish and sprinkle with the walnuts.

DOWNTON PHEASANT CASSEROLE

(serves 4)

Fans of *Downton Abbey* will remember the second season show where the Grantham family and distinguished guests went out on one of the annual pheasant hunts. This was, and still is, a very popular ritual for the English aristocrats. After the hunt, there was a garden party featuring some great dishes and starring the pheasants that were hunted. This dish would have been one of those presented.

Quite obviously you cannot walk into a typical American market and buy pheasant, so Chef Larry Edwards has adapted this dish for today's kitchen and substituted the pheasant with chicken. The only real taste difference is that pheasant is slightly more gamey in taste. If you do want to be totally authentic, you can purchase pheasant from various butchers via the Internet.

Each abbey had its own version of this dish and each featured the fresh products produced at the abbey. This is one of the more "earthier" meals presented at the abbey during this period, and though pheasant would often grace the holiday tables at the abbeys, this dish was only prepared for garden festivities.

Ingredients needed to make Downton Pheasant Casserole:

1 chicken, cut into serving pieces

2 Tbs. flour

salt and black pepper to taste

¼ cup vegetable oil

¼ pound smoked bacon, chopped

4 carrots, peeled and thickly sliced

2 parsnips, peeled and thickly sliced

1 onion, peeled and sliced

2 Tbs. brown sugar

¾ cup hearty red wine

2 cups chicken stock

Steps:

1. Preheat the oven to 350°F.

2. Wipe the chicken pieces of any excess moisture.

3. In a small bowl, whisk together the flour, salt, and black pepper. Dredge (coat) the chicken pieces with the flour mixture.

4. In a large sauté pan, heat the oil over medium heat. Add the chicken and brown on all sides. Remove the chicken and set it aside.

5. Remove and discard the excess oil from the pan (do not rinse the pan out). Place the pan back onto the heat, add the bacon, and sauté 5 minutes.

6. Add the carrots, parsnips, and onions and sauté 5 minutes.

7. Stir into the pan the brown sugar, red wine, and chicken stock. Place the chicken back into the pan.

8. Place a lid on the pan, place into the oven, and cook 75 minutes (1¼ hours).

9. Remove the chicken from the oven. Place the pieces in a large wide bowl. Spoon the vegetables around the chicken and drape with the sauce before serving.

Port Pork Tenderloin

(serves 4)

Whether it be at the abbeys or the palaces of Great Britain, when meat was served as an entrée is was always a good idea to make sure it was fork tender. The thought process behind this is that if you had to use a knife with pressure, the meat could fly off the plate and soil the attire of your guest. This is just one of the reasons why roasts, large fowl, or other such entrées were always sliced very thin. When it came to the cooks preparing pork tenderloin, this was never a problem, as the meat is naturally tender (when prepared properly) and keeps its shape when thinly sliced.

Port Pork Tenderloin was a very proper abbey entrée. Using the pigs they raised on the abbey grounds, their pork was grain-fed and always had a perfect texture. This is one of the few dishes our research found where the cooks actually marinated the meat. It is a very simple marinade, and at the abbeys, it would be marinated at room temperature for one hour. At home in today's kitchen, you can do this part early and marinate it in the refrigerator for up to four hours.

No matter whether you're watching *Downton Abbey* or the numerous Hollywood films of the Victorian and Edwardian era, you always see the aristocrats sipping on port (or sherry). A good port was a staple of the abbeys and often used in the cooking as well. Yet when it was used, the butler of the house oversaw the preparation as he was responsible for all alcohol usage within the abbey.

Ingredients needed to make Port Pork Tenderloin:

1 pound pork tenderloin, trimmed of fat

2½ tsp. salt

½ tsp. ground black pepper

2 cloves garlic, minced

2 Tbs. minced parsley

2 Tbs. olive oil

2 cups sweet sherry

Steps:

1. Rub the pork tenderloin with the salt, black pepper, and garlic. Wrap in plastic wrap and chill 2 hours.

2. Preheat the oven to 350°F.

3. In a medium sauté pan or skillet, heat the olive oil over medium heat. Add the pork tenderloin and brown on all sides (this is called searing the meat). Pour off any rendered fat.

4. With the pan off of the heat, add the sherry.

5. Place in the oven and roast 35 minutes or to desire doneness.

6. Remove from oven and let rest 5 minutes before carving and serving.

Pork Tenderloin with Sweetened Cinnamon Apples

(serves 4)

Along with the pride in their sheep herds, the abbeys also took a great deal of pride in their stable of pigs. There would even be some people from this era who would say the pigs ate better than the townspeople where the abbey was located—and they may be right, as the pigs' diet included many of the leftovers from the dinners served to the guests! For the people outside of the abbey, the prized portion of the pig was the chops. Within the abbey, it was the tenderloin.

When the cooks at the abbey prepared pork tenderloin they removed all the fat with the exception of a very thin layer surrounding the meat. Their reason was they didn't want the pig roasting in its own fat, and it was a fire danger because the ovens, for the most part, were wood burning. Pork Tenderloin with Sweetened Cinnamon Apples is a perfect example of a festive abbey dinner. You have a wonderful and tender piece of meat (sliced very thin upon presentation), a perfect subtle spiciness with the cinnamon, and a hint of sweetness with the apples.

Depending on the abbey and relationship between the lord and his staff, this dish was often allowed to be prepared for the staff on special holidays.

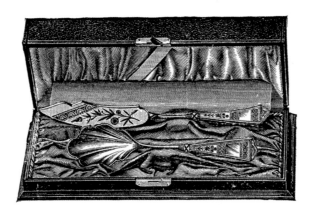

Ingredients needed to make Pork Tenderloin with Sweetened Cinnamon Apples:

1 2-pound pork tenderloin

salt and pepper to taste

1 Tbs. Worcestershire sauce

¼ cup butter

3 Tbs. brown sugar

1 tsp. ground cinnamon

3 apples, cored, peeled, and thinly sliced

Steps:

1. Preheat the oven to 375°F.

2. If needed, remove any excess fat from the pork tenderloin.

3. Season the tenderloin with salt and pepper and rub it with Worcestershire sauce.

4. Place the pork tenderloin in a small roasting pan, place into the oven, and roast 40 minutes.

5. In a medium sauté pan over medium heat, combine the butter, brown sugar, and cinnamon and stir until the butter begins to bubble.

6. Add the apples to the pan and toss to coat.

7. Reduce the heat to low and let cook 10 minutes. The apples will be releasing their juices and creating a natural sauce.

8. Remove the pork tenderloin from the oven and place on a carving board. Let sit 5 minutes.

9. Slice the pork tenderloin thinly.

10. Line a serving platter with the apples and place the pork tenderloin atop. Drizzle with the sauce and serve.

ROYAL OYSTER LOAF

(serves 4)

Surrounding Great Britain you have the Atlantic Ocean, the North Sea, and the English Channel, so one might wonder why during the Edwardian era seafood was not as popular as it might have been at the abbeys. The easy answer to this is it was a commoner's food and the lords and ladies had a reputation to uphold. When seafood was served at the abbeys, it was usually a memorable dish such as this Royal Oyster Loaf.

When the cooks of the abbeys prepared this dish it was done one of two ways: It was either made as individual servings or it was made to be carved and served. If the dinner included special guests, it would be individual and served as one of three courses. If the dinner was just family, it was made larger, portioned at the table, and would be the only course aside from dessert.

At the abbey, only freshly shucked oysters were used for this dish. Because fresh oysters cannot be found in every market today, the whole oysters that come in jars can be used. The bread bowl for this dish was made from scratch at the abbey. They simply made the breads they were used to making yet as small loaves. A perfect bread for this would be Abbey Country Wheat Bread (the recipe in this section). You can also buy small individual round loaves at most markets with a bakery section.

Ingredients needed to make Royal Oyster Loaf:

1 round loaf of bread (or four small ones for individual servings)

¼ cup melted butter

1 pound oyster meat (this does not include the weight of the shell)

1½ cups dry bread crumbs

3 eggs, beaten

2 Tbs. heavy cream

1 cup grated Cheddar cheese

1 lemon, juice only

vegetable oil for frying

Steps:

1. Preheat the oven to 350°F.

2. Slice off the top (crown) of the bread and set aside. Remove the innards (dough) of the bread to leave a shell. Make sure the bread is stable as this will be filled.

3. Brush the inside of the bread with the melted butter.

4. Place the bread into the oven and bake (toast) 10 minutes.

5. Remove the bread from the oven and set aside.

6. If the oysters are the jar variety, pat them dry. If they are freshly shucked, check to make sure no shells are in the crevices of the meat.

7. Dredge (coat) the oysters in the dried bread crumbs.

8. In a small bowl, whisk the eggs and cream.

9. Dip the dredged oysters in the egg mixture and then dredge once again in the bread crumbs.

10. In a medium sauté pan, heat 1 inch of oil over medium heat.

11. Carefully add the oysters and fry a few minutes per side until they are golden in color.

12. Fill the hollowed bread with a layer of oysters followed with a layer of Cheddar cheese, a layer of oysters, the remaining cheese, and the remaining oysters.

13. Squeeze some lemon juice over the top layer of oysters, put the crown on the bread, and serve.

LOBSTER PUDDING

(serves 4)

This is truly an incredible dish and deserving of its royal status. It does take some time to prepare, but it is indeed time well worth spending—and in case you're wondering, it is not really a pudding, not in the strictest sense. What this is is a layered dish encased within a shell of shaved cured ham and prepared as individual servings. When presented at the table, it lays upon a bed of greens and when the guest cuts into it, he or she is met with shards of lobster, the slight sweetness of parsnips, the savory of leeks, and the elegant texture of a bread-crumb pudding.

When this dish was prepared at the abbeys, the cook would shell a whole lobster and then chop up the meat and the coral (often referred to as the "gunk"). Nothing but the shell went to waste. As the dish became popular, certain adaptations were made and this recipe is one of those adaptations. It should be pointed out that steamed dishes were very popular during the Edwardian era and detested by the abbey cooks, as the steaming process would create even more heat within the kitchen, which had no form of ventilation.

The only thing special you will need to prepare this dish is a large steamer and large individual ramekin cups. This dish does call for shaved ham and it is important to the dish. Because most kitchens today do not have a smoke room attached, you can go to a deli and have them slice some cured ham as thin as possible.

Ingredients needed to make Lobster Pudding:

2 lobster tails, shell removed (your butcher can do this for you) and the meat chopped.

¼ cup butter

1 Tbs. Worcestershire sauce

1 parsnip, peeled and julienned

1 leek, thinly sliced (tender white portion only)

½ cup dry bread crumbs

2 eggs, beaten

1 Tbs. heavy cream

¼ pound shaved cured ham

¼ cup sour cream

1 Tbs. horseradish

oil for brushing the ramekin

Steps:

1. In a large sauté pan, melt the butter into the Worcestershire sauce over medium heat. Add the lobster and sauté for 2 minutes. With a slotted spoon, remove the lobster and set aside.

2. Add the parsnip and leek and sauté 5 minutes. Remove the pan from the heat and set aside.

3. In a small bowl, stir together the bread crumbs, eggs, and heavy cream.

4. Lightly brush the bottom and sides of the ramekins with oil.

5. Line the ramekins with the shaved ham. You will want to overlap the sides so when filled you can fold them over to encase the dish.

6. Into the ham-lined ramekins, layer the sautéed vegetable and the lobster. Start with a layer of sautéed vegetable followed by lobster and continue layering ending with lobster. Don't be afraid to pack it down tightly with your hands.

7. Top the lobster layering with the bread crumb mixture.

8. Fold the overlapping shaved cured ham over the lobster pudding and set aside 10 minutes to rest.

9. Fill a steam pot with water and bring to a boil.

10. Into the steaming basket place the lobster pudding. Lower the heat to simmer, cover the pot, and steam 40 minutes. Depending on the size of the steaming baskets, this may have to be done in batches.

11. In a small bowl, whisk together the sour cream and horseradish until smooth.

12. Remove the lobster pudding from the steamer and let sit 5 minutes.

13. Invert (turn over) the ramekin into a serving plate lined with greens.

14. Top with a dollop of the horseradish cream and serve.

LEEK PIE

(serves 4)

When dinner at the abbey was an informal affair it was almost like a day off for the cook and the kitchen staff. It was also a day for the family to enjoy an old-fashioned English dinner without any pomp-and-circumstance, and one of the favorite dishes was the classic Leek Pie. Here, we have two of the most popular food staples of the Edwardian era in one simple to prepare and delightful to eat dish.

Quite obviously, when this dish was prepared at the abbey, the crust for this pie was made from scratch. The recipe for the crust used will be included here but you can also use a prepared one from the supermarket. As far as the leeks go, you only want to use the tender white portions for this pie. The tougher green portions can be used to garnish the dish upon presentation. At the abbeys the tough green portions of the leek would always be saved and used in the various stocks.

If this dish was presented as a side dish, it would be sliced into thin wedges. If presented at an informal family dinner, each serving would be a quarter of the pie and served with a myriad of fresh seasonal fruit.

Ingredients needed to make Leek Pie:

¼ cup butter

4 leeks, tender white portions only

½ tsp. salt

1 cup grated Cheddar cheese

Ingredients needed to make the Pie Crust:

1¼ cups flour

1 tsp. sugar

½ tsp. salt

½ cup butter, chilled and diced

2 Tbs. cold water

Steps:

The Crust:

1. In a large bowl, whisk together the flour, sugar and salt. Add the butter and cut it into the flour with a pastry blender or pastry fork until it resembles coarse crumb, (crumbly). Stir in the water.

2. Place the dough on a floured surface and knead just until the dough comes together (if necessary, add another tablespoon of cold water).

3. Wrap the dough in plastic wrap and chill 30 minutes.

4. Preheat the oven to 350°F.

5. Place the dough on a floured surface and roll out to fit an 8-inch pie pan or dish.

6. Place the rolled out dough into the pie pan. Overlap it slightly as the crust will shrink a bit during baking.

7. Prick the crust all over with the tines of a fork. Place into the oven and bake for 25 minutes.

8. Remove from the oven and let cool.

The Leek Pie Filling:

1. Lower the temperature of the oven to 325°F.

2. In a large sauté pan, melt the butter over medium heat.

3. Add the leeks and salt and sauté 10 minutes.

4. Spoon the sautéed leeks into the pie shell.

5. Layer the top of the leeks with the Cheddar cheese.

6. Place the pie into the oven and bake 20 minutes.

7. Remove from the oven and let cool slightly before cutting and serving.

Whitefish in Cream

(serves 4)

The most useless word in the culinary world is "whitefish." Why? Because there is no such creature. What is meant by "whitefish" is a cold water fish with a white meat. The most common of these would be cod, haddock, whiting, hake, and pollock. Luckily for the cooks at the abbeys, these fish were readily available from the fish mongers in town, and this dish was always a welcome addition to any dinner table.

When the cooks prepared this dish they would use the whole fish. They would skin it and portion it into quarter-pound pieces (a serving size). They would then methodically remove the bones. Once boned, the cook would have two other assistants go over the fish to ascertain all bones were removed. If a portion of fish was served with a bone intact, the cook could be fired on the spot as the bone could cause a guest or family member to choke.

If, per chance, you are not a fan of whitefish, you could prepare this dish using a poached salmon or poached trout. Simply poach the fish as usual and use this sauce to drape over it. Both were seafood favorites at the abbeys.

Ingredients needed to make Whitefish in Cream:

2 Tbs. butter

¼ cup olive oil

2 onions, peeled and thinly sliced

1 pound white fish, sectioned into
   quarter-pound pieces

4 green onions, chopped

¼ cup chopped parsley

½ cup heavy cream

½ tsp. sweet paprika

1 carrot, peeled and thinly sliced

Steps:

1.   In a medium sauté pan, melt the butter into the olive oil over medium heat. Add the onions and sauté for 7 minutes.

2.   Place the fish into the pan, cover, and cook for 10 minutes.

3. In a small bowl, whisk the green onions, parsley, heavy cream, and paprika until smooth.

4. Spoon the cream sauce over the fish, lower the heat to simmer, and cook for 5 minutes.

5. Remove the fish to serving plates, drape with sauce, top with the raw carrot, and serve.

Orange Glazed Beef Brisket

(serves 4)

During the Edwardian era this was probably the most popular cut of beef in England. At the abbeys, it was the second most popular cut behind the standing rib roast, also now known as prime rib. Most people will know beef brisket by another name . . . corned beef! The only difference is the meat is not corned (cured).

Due to citrus fruit being very expensive during the Victorian and Edwardian eras, this dish was reserved for very special occasions. It was also a very popular dish for the cooks as the long cooking period (3 hours) availed them a little time to take a break and enjoy a cup or two of tea. The reason for the long cooking time is to break down the fibers of the beef and make it fork tender.

As with most dishes of this ilk, the meat was sliced in the kitchen before being taken to the dining room. This was also one of the very few dishes where the side dish was included on the same serving platter as the entrée. In today's world, this might be called a "one-pot-dinner."

Ingredients needed to make Orange Glazed Beef Brisket:

1 4-pound beef brisket, trimmed of excess fat

⅓ cup orange juice

¼ cup brown sugar

½ tsp. cornstarch

1 Tbs. butter

1 tsp. grated orange zest

1 pound carrots, peeled and julienned

1 onion, peeled and cut into 8 wedges

Steps:

1. Preheat the oven to 350°F.
2. Place the beef brisket into a large sauté pan and cover with water. Place a lid on the pan, place into the oven and cook 3 hours.

3. In a medium sauté pan over medium heat, stir the orange juice, brown sugar and cornstarch until the cornstarch has dissolved. Bring to a boil and cook two minutes. Remove the pan from the heat and stir in the butter and orange zest.

4. In a small saucepan of boiling water, add the carrots and cook 7 minutes. Add the onion and cook 5 minutes. Remove the vegetables and discard the cooking liquid.

5. Preheat the broiler.

6. Remove the beef brisket from the oven and place on a broiling pan. Brush the beef brisket with some of the orange sauce.

7. Place the beef brisket under the broiler and broil 4 minutes per side.

8. Place the pan with the orange sauce over medium heat, add the carrots and onion, and cook 7 minutes.

9. Remove the beef brisket from the broiler, place on a carving board, and let rest 5 minutes.

10. Carve the beef brisket into thin slices and place on a serving platter. Surround the meat with the vegetables, drape with the orange sauce, and serve.

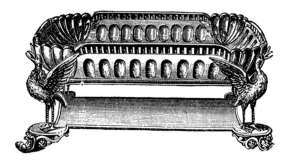

Steamed Fish with Leek Sauce

(serves 4)

To properly and authentically prepare this dish you will need fresh sea bass. If you can't find sea bass, any type of strong fleshy fish will suffice. You need a fleshy fish as the long steaming process will cause more tender fish to fall apart. This dish also calls for fish stock. At the abbey, the cook would make this from the bones and skin of the fish being used. To ease and simplify things, you can use a good quality fish stock from the market.

Leek sauce was one of the most popular cream sauces during the Edwardian era. Its delicate nature and quaint taste was perfect for fish and vegetables. It was also used to top the numerous savory puddings served for dinners or social gatherings. Interesting to note is that even though it is considered a cream sauce, it contains no cream. It gets its consistency and texture from the pureed potatoes and leeks.

If you want to make your own easy fish stock for this dish simply place the skin and bones of the fish into a small saucepan with 2 cups of water, a few black peppercorns, and the greens from the leek. Bring to a boil then reduce the heat to a simmer and cook 15 minutes. Strain the liquid through a fine sieve and discard the solids.

Ingredients needed to make Steamed Fish with Leek Sauce:

1 leek, tender white part only and thinly sliced

1 potato, peeled and sliced

½ cup fish stock

1 Tbs. lemon juice

1 Tbs. butter

2 Tbs. minced dill

1 tsp. minced thyme

¼ tsp. ground white pepper

1 pound sea bass in quarter-pound pieces

1 tsp. salt

½ tsp. ground black pepper

Steps:

1. In a medium saucepan, bring 4 cups of water to a boil. Add the leek and potato, cover, and cook 10 minutes.

2. With a slotted spoon remove the leek and potato and place into a food processor with the fish stock, lemon juice, butter, dill, thyme, and white pepper and puree. Pour the puree into a bowl and set aside.

3. In a steamer, bring 3 cups of water to a boil

4. Season the fish with the salt and pepper. Place the fish into the steamer basket, cover, and steam 10 minutes.

5. Place the fish onto a serving platter, drape with sauce, and serve.

PORK LOAF WITH APPLES

(serves 4)

Prepared mostly to celebrate a holiday or festive occasion, Pork Loaf with Apples was always a proven dish to bring a smile to the creased lips of a Dowager Countess. It is an absolutely succulent dish that features layers of ground pork and beef interspersed with slightly tangy green apples. This was also one of the tallest dishes to ever grace an abbey dining room table.

At the abbeys, the meat was always ground by hand and extra fat was added for both taste and moisture. If you choose to make this dish at home with store-bought ground pork and beef, make sure you get a high-fat variety. If not, it will be too dry and not hold up upon presentation. You can also ask the butcher to add some fat.

You can use any type of apple to prepare this dish. The green apple (Granny Smith) was chosen because an apple too sweet would take away from the taste of the meat.

When presented at the table by the footman, the guest would have his or her choice of sauces to drape over the loaf. In testing this dish, we tried many of those sauces and found them all to overpower the dish. If you did want a sauce, I recommend a simple sour cream and horseradish sauce (¼ cup sour cream blended with 1 tablespoon horseradish).

Ingredients needed to make Pork Loaf with Apples:

1 egg, beaten

1 pound ground beef

1 pound ground pork

1 onion, peeled and chopped

3 carrots, peeled and grated

1 Tbs. cornstarch

2 tsp. salt

½ tsp. ground ginger

1 cup cold water

3 green apples, cored, peeled, and thinly sliced

1 Tbs. butter, chilled and diced

Steps:

1. Preheat the oven to 375°F.

2. In a large bowl, combine all of the ingredients, except the apples and butter, and mix with your hands until very well blended.

3. Lightly brush a 1½-quart casserole dish with oil. Line the bottom with a layer of apples and then spread half the meat mixture on top. Add another layer of apples followed by the remaining meat mixture and top it with the rest of the apples.

4. Dot the top of the loaf with the butter.

5. Place into the oven and bake 80 minutes.

6. Remove from the oven and let rest 10 minutes before serving.

Mutton Pie

(serves 4)

Mutton Pie is a classic English dish that was enjoyed by all classes of people. The reason mutton was used instead of lamb (mutton being aged sheep and a lamb being less than a year old) was that mutton stews better and has a fuller lamb taste. For many palates, mutton is gamey, so if you fit into that category, use lamb. When the cooks of the abbey would prepare this dish, there were two options. The first was a puff pastry topping. The second, which was reserved for special guests and occasions, was what is referred to as a crown. For this dish, I have chosen a crown.

A crown topping is basically a very rich mashed potato whipped with eggs and then piped atop the Mutton Pie. It does take a little more work, but the presentation is well worth it. Once the crown is in place, it can be served as is or you can place it in the oven to add some color to the crown. When the abbey cook would prepare this with a crown, he or she wanted the crown to be white and pure, thus no color was added.

The recipe for the crust of the Mutton Pie is the same recipe used for the Leek Pie, and you can find that recipe in this section.

Ingredients needed to make Mutton Pie:

¼ cup vegetable oil

1 pound lamb meat, diced

¼ cup flour

½ tsp. salt

1½ tsp. ground black pepper

¼ tsp. ground allspice

1 onion, peeled and chopped

1 parsnip, peeled and chopped

1 carrot, peeled and chopped

¼ cup red wine vinegar

½ cup red wine

1 slice of lemon

2 potatoes, diced

1 Tbs. cream

1 Tbs. butter

1 egg, beaten

Steps:

1.   Make your pastry crust the same way as described in the Leek Pie recipe in this section.

2. In a medium sauté pan, heat the oil over medium heat.

3. Carefully add the lamb meat to the pan, sprinkle with the flour, and brown the meat. With a slotted spoon remove the meat and set aside.

4. Add the salt, pepper, allspice, onion, parsnip, and carrot to the pan and sauté 5 minutes.

5. Into the pan pour the vinegar and deglaze the pan with a wooden spoon (scraping the bottom of the pan).

6. Put the lamb back to the pan and add the red wine, bring to a simmer, and cook 10 minutes.

7. Preheat the oven to 350°F.

8. Remove the lamb mixture from the heat and let cool 10 minutes (it will begin to thicken as it cools).

9. Spoon the lamb mixture into the prepared pie crust, place the lemon slice in the middle, and place in the oven to bake 30 minutes.

10. In a medium pot of boiling water, add the potatoes and cook 10 minutes or until fork tender.

11. Drain the potatoes and discard the cooking water. Place the potatoes into a food processor with the cream and butter and puree.

12. Spoon the puree into a bowl and fold in the beaten egg.

13. Fill a pastry bag fitted with a large star tip.

14. Remove the Mutton Pie from the oven.

15. Pipe the potatoes through the tip in a series of small stars going around the pie to create a crown effect.

16. Let the pie rest 5 minutes before serving.

Steak and Kidney Pie

(serves 4)

Steak and Kidney Pie is as British as the monarchy itself. It doesn't matter if you were raised a commoner or a member of the royal family, when you were growing up you ate Steak and Kidney Pie, albeit the preparation was different depending on your social status!

A typical Steak and Kidney Pie is entombed in a basic crust—very good but very boring. Boring was not allowed at the abbeys. How the abbey cooks prepared Steak and Kidney Pie gave it a subtle richness and a regal appearance. First, they didn't really make it as a pie. They used either glass custard cups or ramekins that were lined with buttery rich dough (the same dough to make the crust for Leek Pie in this section), so each one was an individual serving. Second, they gave it a festive topping of rich potatoes, the same recipe used for the crown topping on the Mutton Pie (recipe in this section). It is quite an appealing dish to look at and even better to dine upon.

If you want to make this dish as it was originally made throughout Great Britain during the Edwardian era, simply use an 8-inch pie pan or dish and follow the same directions. If you are a little queasy about eating beef kidneys, just leave them out and add more meat.

Ingredients needed to make Steak and Kidney Pie:

1 pound lean beef, diced small

½ pound beef kidneys, rinsed under cold water

½ cup flour

2 Tbs. butter

1 Tbs. vegetable oil

1 large onion, peeled and chopped

2 carrots, peeled and chopped

3 cups beef stock

1 Tbs. honey

1 recipe of pie dough (see Leek Pie recipe in this section)

1 recipe of mashed potato topping (see Mutton Pie recipe in this section)

Steps:

1. In a medium bowl, toss the beef and kidneys with the flour to coat.
2. In a medium sauté pan, melt the butter into the oil over medium heat.
3. Add the beef, kidneys, and remaining flour and brown the meat.
4. Remove the meat with a slotted spoon and set aside.
5. Add the onion and carrots to the pan and sauté for 7 minutes.
6. Return the beef and kidneys to the pan and stir in the beef stock and honey. Bring the mixture to a simmer and cook 35 minutes.
7. Remove the pan from the heat and let it cool 30 minutes (it will thicken).
8. Prepare your crust dough according to the recipe for Leek Pie in this section. Once the dough is made, roll it out and cut it to fit your custard cups or ramekins. Because the dough will shrink upon baking, make sure it overlaps a little.
9. Place the dough-lined cups in a 350°F oven and bake 25 minutes.
10. Remove the crusts from the oven and spoon in the beef filling, filling right up to the rim.
11. Prepare the mashed potato topping just as detailed in the Mutton Pie recipe. Using the same tip in the pastry bag, go around each pie in a wave-like fashion (see the picture below).
12. Place the Steak and Kidney Pies on a baking sheet, place in the oven, and bake 15 minutes or until the topping gets some color.
13. Remove the pies from the oven and let cool about 5 minutes before serving.

Spring Lamb Loaf

(serves 4)

To be honest, I guess you could say this is the Edwardian version of meatloaf! The difference between this meatloaf and the "stuff" called meatloaf is . . . everything! First of all, what we have here is an incredible combination of ground veal and ground lamb, both of which came from the abbey grounds. What holds the meatloaf together is a combination of fresh bread crumbs, Swiss chard, and an egg. It is interesting to note that after this loaf was carved in the kitchen, the cook would drape it with ketchup, or an abbey version of it—a sweetened, rich, pure tomato sauce.

Whereas most meatloaf dishes are formed by hand, this one must be made in a loaf pan. Due to the fact this is a very moist dish, it must be baked in a mold (pan) to hold it together while the ingredients coagulate from the heat of the oven. This is a very simple recipe to prepare and though it might seem like a "commoner" dish, it was indeed served to special guests and dignitaries invited to dine at the abbey.

A side note to this recipe: Should you have any leftover Spring Lamb Loaf, you might try making a sandwich with it using either the Abbey Country Wheat Bread or the Yorkshire Rye Bread (both recipes are in this section under Breads). You will enjoy an absolutely incredible sandwich!

Ingredients needed to make Spring Lamb Loaf:

1 cup fresh bread crumbs
½ cup cold water
1½ pounds ground lamb
½ pound ground veal
1 onion, peeled and chopped
1 cup chopped Swiss chard leaves (no stems)
¼ cup chopped parsley leaves (no stems)
1 egg, beaten
2 tsp. salt
1 tsp. ground black pepper

Steps:

1. Preheat the oven to 350°F. Line the bottom of a 9 × 5 loaf pan with parchment paper and lightly oil the sides.

2. In a large bowl, combine all the ingredients and mix with your hands until very well blended.

3. Spoon the mixture into the prepared pan and even out.

4. Place the pan on a baking sheet, place into the oven, and bake 90 minutes.

5. Remove from the oven and let cool in the pan 10 minutes.

6. Remove the loaf from the pan and onto a carving board. Slice decently thick and serve.

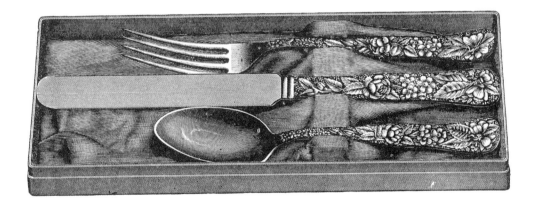

Savory Stuffed Beef Roll

(serves 4)

Whereas meat rolls were considered a peasant food throughout most of Europe during England's Edwardian era, the cooks of the abbeys had a different idea. Like those from the lower classes who made meat rolls as a way to take leftovers to a new eating dimension, at the abbeys it became a gourmet fare. This Savory Stuffed Beef Roll not only shows the culinary genius of the cooks who made it, it also proves that combinations of texture and tastes can make the mouth very happy.

When this meat roll was made at the abbey, it was not made with leftovers. There was no need. The major components of the dish were produced fresh at the abbey—from the beef to the ham to the fresh sausage, it all came from the abbey. An interesting fact about how the cooks prepared the beef: To add a little extra taste and naturally tenderize the beef, they marinated the meat in cider vinegar.

The beef cut for this dish is a sirloin. The meat has to be pounded very thin, but be sure it doesn't tear. If you are somewhat leery about doing this, your butcher should have a machine that will flatten the meat for you.

Ingredients needed to make Savory Stuffed Beef Roll:

1½ pound sirloin beef, ¼-inch thick
before pounding out

¼ cup cider vinegar

2 cloves garlic, minced

1 tsp. ground black pepper

½ pound cured ham, julienned

2 smoked sausages, casing removed and
sliced into rounds

2 hardboiled eggs, shelled and sliced

½ cup chopped green olives

1 cup vegetable oil

1 onion, peeled and chopped

1 bay leaf

2 cups water

1 8-ounce can tomato sauce

2 tsp. salt

2 tomatoes, chopped

Steps:

1. Pound the steak as thin as possible without tearing the meat. Place the meat into a nonmetallic shallow dish and add the vinegar and garlic. Toss the meat to coat and let it marinate at room temperature 30 minutes.

2. Remove the beef from the marinade and pat dry. Reserve the marinade.

3. Place the meat on a flat surface and layer the ham, sausage, and eggs upon the meat. Over this layer sprinkle the olives.

4. Roll the meat up jellyroll-style and tie it with kitchen string making sure both ends are secure.

5. In a large sauté pan, heat the oil over medium heat. Add the beef roll and brown on all sides. Pour out and discard the rendered fat and excess oil.

6. Add the onion, bay leaf, water, tomato sauce, salt, chopped tomatoes, and reserved marinade to the pan. Bring the mixture to a boil and then reduce the heat to a simmer. Cover the pan and cook 90 minutes.

7. Remove the beef roll from the pan and place on a carving board. Snip off the kitchen string and slice the beef roll thickly.

8. Place the beef roll on a serving platter, spoon the sauce atop, and serve.

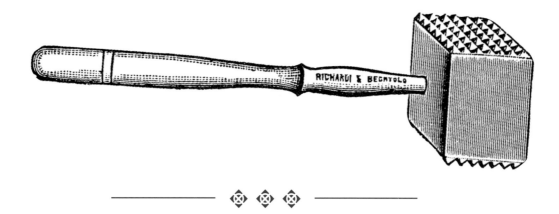

Desserts at the Abbey

❖ ❖ ❖

Queen Victoria Rice Pudding

(serves 4)

Dessert was a special time at the abbeys. It was the culmination of a wonderful dinner. It meant the end of a social day. Though at times there was business discussed during the course of dinner, once dessert was served the mood turned light and gay. The desserts of the abbey were very seldom extra fancy. There were no sculptured cakes or treats only Da Vinci could prepare. It was elegant and it was easy.

This particular rice pudding is not your typical rice pudding. This is rich, elegant, and created with royalty in mind. Whereas the lower class of Edwardian England would dessert with rice pudding, theirs was not laden with heavy cream, fresh exotic spices, and speckled throughout with little ruby-colored red currant gems.

This rice pudding recipe was created for Queen Victoria and since the time it was first served within the walls of her palaces, it has become a staple for elegant dinners parties thrown by aristocrats. Upon being served, Queen Victoria Rice Pudding would be accompanied by a small pitcher or bowl of heavy cream and honey to add even more richness and sweetness.

Ingredients needed to make Queen Victoria Rice Pudding:

4 cups water

2 cups long-grain rice

½ tsp. ground nutmeg

1½ Tbs. ground cinnamon

2 Tbs. butter, softened

4 eggs, beaten

1 Tbs. vanilla

¾ cup sugar

½ cup heavy cream

¼ cup red currants or red currant jelly

Steps:

1. Preheat the oven to 350°F. Lightly oil the bottom and sides of a 1½-quart baking or soufflé dish or small cups for individual servings.

2. In a medium saucepan, bring the 4 cups of water to a boil. Stir in the rice, nutmeg, and cinnamon. Reduce the heat to a simmer, place a lid on the pan, and cook 20 minutes.

3. Remove the pan from the heat and let sit, covered, for 20 minutes.

4. In a medium bowl, whisk the butter, eggs, vanilla, sugar, heavy cream, and red currants until smooth.

5. Spoon the rice into the prepared dish. Pour the cream mixture over the rice and gently stir to blend.

6. Place into the oven and bake 35 minutes.

7. Remove from the oven and let cool slightly before serving.

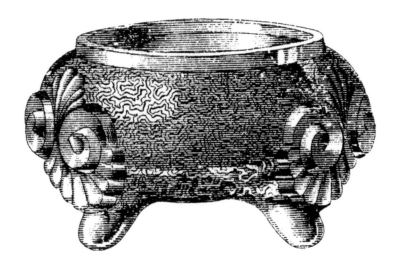

LEMON CRÈME SOUFFLÉ

(makes 4)

As anyone who has a yearning for British cuisine will attest to, the Brits do indeed love lemons and their famed lemon curd. During the Edwardian era, lemons, as well as all citrus fruit, were rather expensive and dishes featuring these fruits were not very common—and almost unheard of in the dining rooms of the "common" people. This dessert soufflé was usually reserved for special occasions at the abbeys. Though it is quite simple to prepare, it does take a few steps.

This dessert exemplifies the brilliance of the abbey cooks. What the cooks did was take a basic lemon curd and give it body in the form of egg whites. Of course, when using egg whites in this way, you get more air into the curd and when air gets hot, it raises what it is mixed with. So, there are other types of lemon soufflé, but probably none as creamy as the ones prepared at the abbeys!

You will need individual soufflé bowls for this dish. They are readily available and inexpensive at all kitchenware stores. Also rather unusual here is the abbey cooks would brush the soufflé bowls with butter before adding the mixture. In most soufflés, you really don't want to do this as you want the egg whites to cling to the bowl while they are rising. Our research shows no reason why the cooks did this. Perhaps it was just to add richness to the dessert.

Ingredients needed to make Lemon Crème Soufflé:

3 Tbs. butter (plus a little extra to brush the bowls)

⅔ cup milk

⅓ cup heavy cream

½ cup sugar

3 egg yolks

1 Tbs. flour

1¼ Tbs. cornstarch

4 egg whites

2 lemons, juice and finely grated zest

powdered sugar for dusting

Steps:

1. Preheat the oven to 400°F.

2. Brush the sides and bottom of the soufflé bowls with a little butter. Set the bowls aside.

3. In a medium saucepan stir the butter, milk, and cream and bring to a simmer over medium heat.

4. In a medium bowl, whisk the egg yolks and sugar until pale and thickened.

5. Whisk the flour and cornstarch into the egg mixture until smooth.

6. Slowly whisk the hot cream mixture into the eggs until well incorporated. Then pour the mixture back into the saucepan and stir 5 minutes or until it thickens. Remove the pan from the heat and let cool.

7. In a mixer with a whisk attachment, beat the egg whites until stiff peaks form.

8. Stir the lemon juice and zest into the cream mixture.

9. Stir one-third of the egg whites into the cream mixture until combined. Fold in the remaining egg whites.

10. Spoon the mixture into the prepared soufflé bowls.

11. Place the soufflés onto a baking sheet. Place into the oven and bake 15 minutes (do not open the oven door during this time).

12. Remove from the oven, dust with some powdered sugar, and serve.

DEVONSHIRE STRAWBERRY SHORTCAKE

(serves 4)

Don't let the title of this dessert fool you. This is probably unlike any other strawberry shortcake you have ever eaten. First, you have an authentic English shortcake. Very rich and very tender. Second, you are enveloping the strawberries with a mixture of heavy cream and Devonshire cream. This is strawberry shortcake before it was ruined by being cute and artsy.

This dessert was one of the most popular at the abbeys and served year-round. When strawberries weren't in season, the cook would simply substitute another seasonal berry. This was also a very popular lunch dish at the abbeys and, in a few episodes of *Downton Abbey*, you can see it being served in the family dining room during the midafternoon meal.

To purchase Devonshire cream outside of Great Britain is not really that difficult. Most markets that have international food sections will carry it, and it can always be found via the Internet. It is a very rich "coddled" cream and blends wonderfully with the heavy cream for this dessert.

Ingredients needed to make Devonshire Strawberry Shortcake:

1 cup flour

¾ cup cornstarch

½ tsp. salt

½ cup butter, softened

½ cup sugar

1 egg, beaten

¼ cup heavy cream

⅔ cup Devonshire cream

¼ cup powdered sugar

2 tsp. vanilla

3 cups strawberries, hulled and quartered

Steps:

1. In a small bowl, whisk together the flour, cornstarch and salt.

2. In a mixer with a paddle attachment, beat the butter, sugar, and egg until smooth.

3. With the mixer on low speed, add the flour mixture and beat just until it forms a dough.

4. Wrap the dough in plastic and chill 30 minutes.

5. Preheat the oven to 325°F. Line a baking sheet with parchment paper or a silicon sheet.

6. Place the dough on a floured surface and roll out to ⅛-inch thickness. Using a round biscuit or cookie cutter, cut out rounds. You will need eight, two for each dessert. (If you have extra, store in an airtight container for a few days.)

7. Place the shortcakes on the prepared cookie sheet and bake 25 minutes.

8. Remove from the oven and let cool on a wire rack.

9. In a large bowl, whisk together the heavy cream, Devonshire cream, powdered sugar, and vanilla until soft peaks form.

10. Place the strawberries into the bowl and fold them into the cream.

11. Spoon some Devonshire Strawberries over a piece of the shortcake, top with another piece of shortcake, and serve.

GRANTHAM STEAMED ORANGE MARMALADE PUDDING

(serves 4)

In the culinary world, Europe holds the crown for the most dessert puddings created. A few major jewels in that crown belong to England, a country that has shared with the world many great puddings including this classic perfected during the Victorian era and extremely popular during the Edwardian era. Next to the famed plum pudding, a favorite of the Dowager Countess Violet Grantham, this pudding may be the second most popular to ever come out of England.

This pudding has been adapted for today's kitchen and to pay homage to *Downton Abbey*, Chef Larry Edwards has named the pudding after the abbey's family, the Granthams. Whereas most American types of pudding are creamy in texture, English ones have more of a body and are often quite sticky. This is a very simple dessert to prepare but it will take some time to complete as it is a steamed pudding and steaming takes more time than baking.

Arguably the best marmalades in the world come from England, yet the oranges used are not British at all. The common orange used to make English marmalade are Seville oranges from Spain!

Ingredients needed to make Grantham Steamed Orange Marmalade Pudding:

½ cup orange marmalade

⅔ cup butter, softened

2 Tbs. corn syrup

1 orange, zest only and finely grated

¾ cup sugar

3 eggs, beaten

2 Tbs. milk

½ cup flour

2 tsp. baking powder

Steps:

1. In a large steamer, bring 4 cups of water to a boil and then lower the heat to simmer.

2. Lightly oil the sides of four ramekins and spoon a teaspoon of marmalade into the bottoms.

3. In a mixer with a paddle attachment, beat the butter, corn syrup, orange zest, and sugar until smooth.

4. Beat in the eggs, one at a time, until fully incorporated.

5. Beat in the milk and remaining marmalade until creamy.

6. Sift the flour and baking powder over the dry ingredients and then fold it in to make a smooth batter.

7. Spoon the mixture into the prepared ramekins.

8. Place the ramekins into a steaming basket (in batches if necessary) and steam 45 minutes.

9. Remove the pudding from the steamer and serve.

Downton Pound Cake

(makes 1 cake)

Every abbey had its own version of pound cake. For many of the abbeys the originality of its pound cake was almost as important as the family crest. Because Downton Abbey is a fictional abbey, Chef Larry Edwards created a special pound cake that is as rich as Downton Abbey, as noble as a lord, as sweet as a lady and has a slight touch of sass to pay homage to the Dowager Countess.

The pound cake was the most popular dessert item at an abbey. It was served year-round in one form or another. During the spring and summer months it was always accompanied by either fresh fruit or a freshly made fruit compote. During the fall and winter, it was served with either a Devonshire cream or an assortment of flavored whipped creams. For the abbey dining room, the cake was always baked in a mold, usually a bundt mold. For the staff, the pound cake was always baked in a loaf pan. During the holidays, this pound cake would be draped with dark chocolate and scattered with slivered almonds.

The original name of pound cake derives, according to culinary lore, from its original recipe involving a pound of butter, a pound of flour, a pound of eggs, and a pound of sugar!

Ingredients needed to make Downton Pound Cake:

3 cups flour

½ tsp. salt

¼ tsp. baking powder

1 cup butter, softened

3 cups sugar

6 eggs, separated

1 Tbs. vanilla

1 Tbs. almond extract

Steps:

1. Preheat the oven to 350°F. Lightly brush a bundt cake pan with oil or use a cooking spray.

2. In a medium bowl, whisk together the flour, salt, and baking powder. Set the bowl aside.

3. In a mixer with a paddle attachment, beat the butter and sugar until light and pale.

4. Beat in the egg yolks, vanilla, and almond extract until smooth.

5. Add the flour mixture and beat just until combined.

6. In a separate bowl, whisk the egg whites until stiff peaks form.

7. Remove half of the egg whites and stir them into the pound cake batter. Fold the other half of the egg whites into the batter.

8. Spoon the batter into the prepared pan.

9. Place into the oven and bake 70 minutes or until a tester comes out clean.

10. Remove the cake from the oven and let cool in the pan 10 minutes.

11. Remove the cake from the pan and let cool on a wire rack until ready to serve.

Note: If you want to do the holiday version, simply melt some dark chocolate with a touch of butter and drape it along the top of the cake, letting it run down the sides, and scatter some slivered almonds.

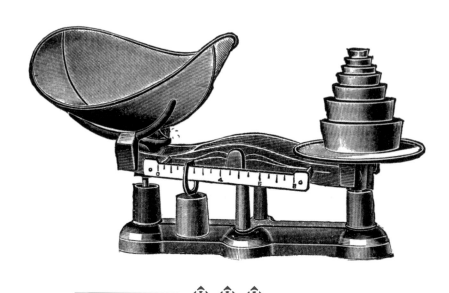

Raspberry Nut Sponge Cake

(makes 1 cake)

In doing the research on this cake, I came across some notes from an abbey cook who made this cake into a wedding cake for one of the ladies of her house. I shook my head in wonderment. This is an incredibly fragile cake and to think of it being a seven-layer wedding cake boggled my mind. How fragile is this cake? It only has ⅓ cup of flour to bring the cake together. The rest of the texture is the ground nuts and egg whites!

This cake calls for raspberry preserves. At the abbeys, they made their own with freshly harvested raspberries. If you buy a commercial variety, make sure it is pure and not a jam or jelly. This is very important to the flavor of the cake, and anything but a natural preserve can cause the cake to become too moist and fall apart when you slice it.

Often times, Raspberry Nut Sponge Cake was served just as you see in the picture. On rare occasions, the guest would have the option of a dollop of some freshly whipped cream or Devonshire cream. On very special occasions, it would be served with a pure raspberry syrup laced with a raspberry liqueur.

Ingredients needed to make Raspberry Nut Sponge Cake:

7 Tbs. butter, softened

⅓ cup powdered sugar

4 eggs, separated

⅓ cup finely ground almonds

⅓ cup flour

2 tsp. cream of tartar

1 tsp. baking soda

½ cup pure raspberry preserves

Steps:

1. Preheat the oven to 350°F. Line the bottom of two 8-inch round cake pans with parchment paper.

2. Into a mixer with a paddle attachment beat the butter and powdered sugar until light.

3. Beat in the egg yolks and almonds until very well blended.

4. Stir—do not beat—the flour, cream of tartar, and baking soda into the cream mixture.

5. In a medium bowl, whisk the egg whites until stiff peaks form.

6. Fold the egg whites into the batter.

7. Divide the batter between both prepared cake pans.

8. Place in the oven and bake 20 minutes.

9. Remove from the oven and let cool in the pan 10 minutes.

10. Remove the cakes from the pan and let cool on a wire rack.

11. When cool, spread the raspberry preserves on the top of one of the cakes.

12. Place the second cake atop the raspberry preserved layered first cake.

13. Chill the cake until ready to slice and serve.

Chocolate-Laced Flat Cakes

(serves 4)

You are going to make an English version of crepes for this dessert. Don't worry, it's easy. You can make the crepes ahead of time and keep them fresh by placing them between sheets of waxed paper in a sealable plastic bag in the refrigerator.

Chocolate-Laced Flat Cakes may be the epitome of an elegant chocolate dessert. Prepared at the abbey for special occasions and honored guests, this dessert features a dark rich chocolate with a cocoa index of 80 percent. It is almost pure chocolate! To make it even more special and elegant, the chocolate is laced with brandy!

The abbey cook would prepare the crepes the morning the dinner they would be served. Because there was no refrigeration at the abbeys during the Edwardian era, the crepes would be kept moist by constantly having a hot towel wrapped around them. The chocolate mixture would be prepared only minutes before the dish was to leave the kitchen for the dining room, and would be made under the watchful eye of the house butler because there was liquor involved.

Ingredients needed to make Chocolate-Laced Flat Cakes:

2 eggs, beaten

2 cups milk

1½ cups flour

1 Tbs. sugar

1 tsp. salt

vegetable oil for brushing the crepe pan

8-ounces dark chocolate of high cocoa index

1 Tbs. brandy

2 Tbs. heavy cream

Steps:

1. In a medium bowl, whisk together the eggs, milk, flour, sugar, and salt until you have a smooth batter. Set the bowl aside 15 minutes.

2. Heat a crepe pan over medium heat and brush with oil.

3. Re-whisk the crepe batter. Spoon enough batter to cover the bottom of the crepe pan and once you start to see bubbles, turn the crepe over and cook 1 minute. Repeat this step with the remaining batter.

4. Cool the crepes between sheets of waxed paper. The crepes must be totally cooled to proceed.

5. In a small heat-proof bowl over simmering water (or a double-boiler), melt the chocolate until smooth and creamy.

6. Whisk the brandy and heavy cream into the chocolate until smooth.

7. Fold the crepes into quarters and layer them on a serving platter.

8. Spoon the chocolate atop the crepes and serve.

COTTAGE CHEESE CAKE

(makes 1 cake)

A very popular cheesecake during the Victorian and Edwardian era, Cottage Cheese Cake employs one of England's most popular cheeses. Where cottage cheese was originated can be debated, but it is known that the term was created in 1848 to describe the cheese curd made in the cottages of the English countryside. At the abbeys, they made their own cottage cheese using the leftover milk from their daily churning of butter.

To make the task of preparing this cheese cake easier, use a small curd cottage cheese and drain it through a fine sieve. You just want the curd and as little of the whey (liquid) as possible. Because the curd will be creamed, small curds make that task much faster and easier. This is a very easy cheesecake to prepare at home, though it might seem strange that this cheesecake is crustless. What happens during the baking process is that the cheesecake will create its own crust. The only special item you'll need to prepare Cottage Cheese Cake is a springform pan.

Just as if you were employed as part of the kitchen staff at Downton Abbey, you will want to present your Cottage Cheese Cake slightly chilled and place in the middle a peeled, cored, and thinly sliced flared pear.

Ingredients needed to make Cottage Cheese Cake:

4 cups small curd cottage cheese, drained through a fine sieve

8 eggs, beaten

½ tsp. salt

1 Tbs. cornstarch

¼ cup white cornmeal

2 Tbs. butter, softened

1 cup sour cream

1½ cups sugar

1 pear, cored, peeled, and thinly sliced

Steps:

1. Preheat the oven to 350°F. Line the bottom of a 9-inch springform pan with parchment paper.

2. In a mixer with the paddle attachment, beat the cottage cheese until smooth. This will take a few minutes.

3. Beat the eggs into the cheese until light and pale.

4. Add the salt, cornstarch, cornmeal, butter, sour cream, and sugar and beat until smooth and creamy.

5. Pour the batter into the prepared pan.

6. Place in the oven and bake 90 minutes.

7. Turn the oven off, but do not remove the cheesecake. Let the cheesecake cool in the oven until you can reach in and take it out with your bare hands.

8. Remove the cheesecake and let it cool to room temperature.

9. Flare the pear atop the cheesecake and chill until ready to slice and serve.

Spiced Caramel Apple Crepes

(serves 4)

Before the Edwardian era, there was the Victorian era. Queen Victoria loved caramel and toffee. As a matter of fact, long before today's salted caramel craze, the cooks of the abbeys were preparing it for a multitude of sweet dishes. To this day, you can find tins of both with the queen's almost-smiling face etched on the tins.

There are a few steps to this dish. You must make some crepes and you can use the same recipe as in Chocolate-Laced Flat Cakes (located in this section). Then, you must make the caramel sauce. A very easy recipe that requires no candy thermometer. Then, you prepare the apples, after which you put the dish together.

As with any type of crepe dish, you can make the crepes ahead of time. With this dish you can also make the caramel sauce ahead of time and if you want it thicker than it is when it is warm, simply chill it for a bit. The final construction of the dessert should occur just before it is presented.

Ingredients needed to make Spiced Caramel Apple Crepes:

2 Granny Smith apples

2 Tbs. butter

¼ cup brown sugar

½ tsp. ground cinnamon

¼ tsp. salt

crepes (see recipe for Chocolate-Laced
    Flat Cakes in this section) caramel sauce
    (recipe to follow)

Ingredients needed to make Caramel Sauce:

¾ cup sugar

1 tsp. sea salt

¼ cup water

1 Tbs. corn syrup

½ cup heavy cream

¼ cup butter

Steps:

1. Peel and core each of the apples. Chop the apples and set them aside. It will be natural for them to turn brown and it won't bother anything. If you don't want this, toss them in a small amount of lemon juice.

2. In a medium sauté pan over medium heat, stir together the butter, brown sugar, cinnamon, and salt and cook just until the butter begins to bubble.

3. Add the apples, toss to coat, and cook 10 minutes.

4. Place the apple mixture in a bowl and set aside to cool.

5. Line up your crepes on a flat surface.

6. Spoon and spread some of the apple mixture over each crepe and then roll the crepes up to envelope the apples.

7. Place the apple-filled crepes on serving dishes, drizzle with the Caramel Sauce, and serve.

Steps for Caramel Sauce:

1. In a medium pot over medium heat, stir the sugar, salt, water, and corn syrup until the sugar dissolved and the liquid is clear.

2. Continue stirring the mixture until it turns amber in color, about 15 minutes.

3. Remove the pot from the heat and slowly and carefully stir in the cream. You will have a minor implosion when the cream hits the amber syrup.

4. Stir in the butter until the caramel is smooth and creamy. As it cools it will thicken.

LEMON CORNMEAL CAKE

(makes 1 cake)

Cornmeal was a popular staple in the kitchens of the abbey yet in all of our research, we couldn't find one single cornbread! The corn for the cornmeal used at the abbeys was grown in the garden and then shipped off to a local miller to be made into cornmeal. For the most part, the cooks used the cornmeal as a thickener for some sauces and soups and sprinkled it on baking pans and stones for bread (the cornmeal acting as a non-stick surface).

Though not fancy by any means, this dessert was indeed special as it contained citrus fruit which was very expensive in England during the Edwardian era. It is a very simple cake to prepare and very reminiscent of a lemony-rich pound cake. The wonderful moistness of this cake is derived from the sour cream and the texture, a slight crunch, from the cornmeal.

Upon presentation at the table, the thickly sliced portions of Lemon Cornmeal Cake were accompanied by either slightly sweetened whipped cream or Devonshire cream. If it was a very special occasion, the cake would be elegantly draped with freshly made lemon curd.

Ingredients needed to make Lemon Cornmeal Cake:

1 cup sugar

1 cup butter, softened

4 eggs

½ cup sour cream

1 lemon, the zest only and finely grated

1¼ cups flour

¾ cup yellow cornmeal

1½ tsp. baking powder

½ tsp. salt

Steps:

1. Preheat the oven to 350°F. Line the bottom of a 9 × 5 loaf pan with parchment paper.

2. In a mixer with the paddle attachment, beat the sugar and butter until light and creamy.

3. Add the eggs, one at a time, and beat until fully incorporated.

4. Add the sour cream and lemon zest and beat 2 minutes.

5. In a medium bowl, whisk together the flour, yellow cornmeal, baking powder, and salt.

6. Stir the dry ingredients into the cream mixture just until it comes together. Over-stirring will cause a dense cake,

7. Spoon the batter into the prepared pan.

8. Place into the oven and bake 60 minutes or until the sides separate from the pan.

9. Remove from the oven and let cool in the pan 5 minutes.

10. Remove from the pan and cool on a wire rack until ready to slice and serve.

Raspberries in Sherry Sabayon Sauce

(serves 4)

This dessert became very popular for festive occasions at the abbeys after World War I ended and the French influence of cooking began to take hold in England. When first incorporated on the menu, it was prepared with a sweet sherry. Once it became a staple, the sweet wine of choice was the old English standby . . . port!

You can use any type of fresh in-season berry for this dish. If it is as larger berry, such as a strawberry, you will want to make sure to cut the fruit small enough where a portion of the fruit will fit into a dessert spoon along with some of the sauce. At the abbeys, this dessert was served for special guests and festivities, thus it was always served in either a crystal goblet or flute style of glass.

This dish does call for a product known as superfine sugar (also found in markets as Baker's Sugar). It is, as you might guess, a finely granulated sugar meant to dissolve quickly. You can make your own by simply putting some sugar into a food processor and giving it a few spins under the blade.

Ingredients needed to make Raspberries in Sherry Sabayon Sauce:

2 cups fresh raspberries	¼ cup sugar
¼ cup superfine sugar	½ cup sherry
2 egg yolks	1 Tbs. grenadine syrup

Steps:

1. Place the berries in a medium bowl and toss with the superfine sugar.

2. In a small saucepan over medium-low heat, whisk the egg yolks and sugar until the color turns pale. You must whisk the entire time or the eggs will scramble.

3. As you are whisking, slowly add the sherry and grenadine syrup until you have a thick and creamy sauce.

4. Spoon the raspberries into the goblets or flutes.

5. Strain the sabayon sauce through the fine sieve to remove any cooked portions of egg.

6. Spoon the sauce over the berries and serve.

Sour Cream Pound Cake

(makes 1 cake)

This Edwardian-era style of pound cake was perfect for the abbeys. It is somewhat more dense in texture than a usual pound cake, thus it was able to be served with a fresh fruit compote or a syrup laden fruit without breaking down or falling apart while it was being served. Pound cakes of various styles were served year-round at the abbeys and their accompaniment was usually decided upon the season.

To give this pound cake the texture it needs to achieve its culinary goal, the usual heavy batter is naturally lightened with beaten egg whites. This gives the cake the ability to rise while baking and the strength to uphold whatever is being served with it. You will notice that as it cools it loses some of its height. This is simply the cake settling and creating its fantastic texture.

If there were leftover portions of this pound cake, the next morning the cook would toast it and it would be served at breakfast with some sweetened creamery-fresh butter and fresh fruit preserves.

Ingredients needed to make Sour Cream Pound Cake:

3 cups flour

½ tsp. salt

¼ tsp. baking soda

1 cup butter, softened

3 cups sugar

6 eggs, separated

2 Tbs. vanilla

1¼ cups sour cream

Steps:

1. Preheat the oven to 350°F. Lightly oil or spray a bundt pan or line the bottoms of two 9 × 5 loaf pans with parchment paper.

2. In a medium bowl, whisk the flour, salt, and baking soda. Set the bowl aside.

3. In a mixer with the paddle attachment, beat the butter and sugar 5 minutes. Add the egg yolks and vanilla and beat until smooth.

4. With the mixer on low, beat in half the flour mixture, followed by the sour cream and then the remaining flour mixture.

5. In a large bowl, whisk the egg white until stiff peaks form.

6. Stir half the beaten egg whites into the batter until combined.

7. Fold the remaining egg whites into the batter.

8. Spoon the batter into the prepared pan.

9. Place in the oven and bake 90 minutes or until the sides break away from the pan.

10. Remove the cake from the oven and let cool in the pan 15 minutes.

11. Remove from the pan and let cool on a wire rack until ready to slice and serve.

Walnut Butter Cake

(makes 1 cake)

I suppose it only makes sense that one of the most requested Edwardian era desserts feature one of the most known English food products, the English walnut. In reality, there is no such nut! What is known as the English walnut is actually a Persian walnut, but the English get credit for it as they were the ones to introduce it to America in the early 1800s. In England, the English walnut is known as the "Common Nut."

Walnut Butter Cake is indeed one of the richer desserts to be presented at the abbey as it features seven egg yolks, a cup of butter, a cup of heavy cream, and the oils of a cup of ground walnuts. When it was served, the guests had their choice of sweetened whipped cream, triple cream, or Devonshire cream to dollop upon their thick slice. In today's world, this would be called a "dieter's nightmare."

On the rare chance any of the cake would make it back to the kitchen after dinner, the abbey cook would make something very special for the staff. The cook would prepare a very simple vanilla custard and once it was chilled, would stir it with cut up portions of the walnut cake for a snack cleverly called "Walnut Butter Cake Custard."

Ingredients needed to make Walnut Butter Cake:

1 cup butter, softened

3 cups sugar

7 eggs

2 tsp. vanilla

1 cup heavy cream

1 cup finely ground walnuts

3 cups flour

1 tsp. salt

powdered sugar for dusting

Steps:

1. Preheat the oven to 350°F. Lightly oil or spray a bundt pan.

2. In a mixer with a paddle attachment, beat the butter and sugar until light and pale.

3. Add the eggs and beat 10 minutes.

4. Add the vanilla, heavy cream, and walnuts and beat 5 minutes.

5. With the mixer on a slow speed, add the flour and salt and beat just until a batter is formed.

6. Spoon the batter into the prepared pan and even out.

7. Place the cake into the oven and bake 80 minutes or until the sides break away from the pan.

8. Remove the cake from the oven and let cool in the pan 10 minutes.

9. Remove the cake from the pan and let cool on a wire rack.

10. Before slicing and serving, dust the cake with powdered sugar.

Sour Cream Spice Cake

(makes 1 cake)

If you've had the pleasure of watching the *Downton Abbey* Christmas Special, you would have noticed that the staff were afforded the pleasure of having their own Christmas party. The kitchen table was laden with food, both savory and sweet. This Sour Cream Spice Cake was the crown of the table. It features the spices of the holiday and a nice slight hint of citrus.

You might also have noticed that most of the pans and molds used to make cakes were of the high variety. This was quite common during both the Victorian and Edwardian eras in England and the reason is that the height and shape were thought to resemble a crown (paying homage to the monarchy). In other parts of Europe, such pans and molds were shorter and wider.

A great misnomer regarding the foods of England is that they are bland. Fact-of-the-matter is, many English dishes, such as this cake, did contain what many considered at the time to be exotic spices. This should not really come as a surprise when you consider that, during this time, the reign of the British monarchy did include many portions of the Asian continent where these spices originate.

Ingredients needed to make Sour Cream Spice Cake:

4 cups flour

1 tsp. baking soda

½ tsp. ground cloves

½ tsp. ground cinnamon

3 eggs, beaten

2½ cups sugar

1½ cups sour cream

2 Tbs. honey

1 cup black currants or raisins

3 Tbs. finely grated orange zest

powdered sugar for dusting

Steps:

1. Preheat the oven to 325°F. Lightly oil or spray a bundt pan.

2. In a medium bowl, whisk together the flour, baking soda, cloves, and cinnamon. Set the bowl aside.

3. In a mixer using a paddle attachment, beat the eggs and sugar until light and pale.

4. Add the sour cream and honey and beat until smooth and creamy.

5. With the mixer on a slow speed, add the flour mixture and beat until it forms a batter.

6. Fold into the batter in the black currants or raisins.

7. Spoon the batter into the prepared pan.

8. Place into the oven and bake 75 minutes or until the sides break away from the pan.

9. Remove the cake from the oven and let cool in the pan 10 minutes.

10. Remove the cake from the pan and let cool on a wire rack.

11. Before slicing and serving, dust the cake with some powdered sugar.

Apple Noodle Pudding

(serves 4)

The abbeys employed many people and they came from all walks of life throughout the countries of Great Britain. When they came to the abbeys they often brought the dishes of their country. At Downton Abbey, you had workers from Ireland, Wales, and Scotland. This dish was brought to the English abbeys from Wales and though it may sound strange, it is actually a very rich and delicious dessert.

Though this is a sweet dessert, the sweetness can be controlled by the type of apple used. The cook at the abbey would determine which type of apple by what the entrée was going to be. If the entrée consisted of lamb or beef, red apples would be used for extra sweetness. If the entrée was pork, seafood, or fowl, a green apple would be used for a slight touch of tartness.

You might be asking yourself, why noodles in a dessert pudding? The origins of this dessert is peasant food and peasants couldn't afford the heavy cream to make actual pudding. The eggs and flour they had in abundance, so they made their own egg noodles and used them to create a faux pudding texture.

Ingredients needed to make Apple Noodle Pudding:

¼ cup butter

4 green apples, peeled, cored, and thinly sliced

3 eggs, separated

¾ cup sugar

¼ tsp. salt

1 tsp. ground cardamom

½ cup red currants or raisins

¼ pound cooked egg noodles

Steps:

1. Preheat the oven to 375°F. Lightly oil the bottom and sides of a 1½-quart ovenproof baking dish.

2. In a large sauté pan, melt the butter over medium heat. Add the apples and sauté 10 minutes. Remove the pan from the heat.

3. In a large bowl, whisk the egg yolks, sugar, salt, and cinnamon until smooth. Stir in the red currants, egg noodles, and apples.

4. In a medium bowl, whisk the egg whites until stiff peaks form. Fold the egg whites into the apple mixture.

5. Spoon the mixture into the prepared baking dish.

6. Place in the oven and bake 35 minutes.

7. Remove from the oven and let cool before serving.

Downton Abbey HONEY CAKE

(makes 1 cake)

Dark, rich, spicy, sweet, and loaded with dried fruits and walnuts, this classic abbey dessert often times represented the family who owned the abbey. Because each abbey had its version of this dessert and Downton Abbey is a fictitious abbey, Chef Larry Edwards has created *Downton Abbey* Honey Cake specifically for this book.

What this particular honey cake is, is an adaptation and combination of other abbey inspired honey cakes. For the rich dark color, the chef uses not only spices, but the inclusion of strong black coffee. For the dried fruits, two of the favorites of the Edwardian era, raisins and apricots and it couldn't be truly English if it did not include English walnuts.

This cake is baked loaf style and upon presentation, it would be brought to the dinner table on a white platter, which showcased its dark and rich color. When not being served as a dessert, this cake would find its way into the abbey's library after a dinner where the gentleman would enjoy a slice with their brandy or whiskey.

Ingredients needed to make *Downton Abbey* **Honey Cake:**

2 eggs, separated

½ cup sugar

½ cup vegetable oil

½ cup pure honey

1½ Tbs. very strong black coffee (espresso may be used)

2 cups flour

1¼ tsp. baking powder

½ tsp. baking soda

½ tsp. ground cinnamon

¼ tsp. ground cardamom

¼ tsp. ground cloves

1 Tbs. finely grated orange zest

¼ cup raisins

¼ cup minced dried apricots

¼ cup minced walnuts

Steps:

1.   Preheat the oven to 350°F. Line the bottom of a 9 × 5 loaf pan with parchment paper.

2. In a mixer with a paddle attachment, beat the egg yolks and sugar until light and pale and then beat in the oil, honey and strong black coffee.

3. In a medium bowl, whisk together the flour, baking powder, baking soda, and all spices.

4. With the mixer on a low speed, gradually add the dry ingredients just until a batter forms.

5. In a medium bowl, whisk the egg whites until stiff peaks form. Stir one-third of the egg whites into the batter and then fold the remaining whites into the batter along with the orange zest, raisins, dried apricots, and walnuts.

6. Spoon the mixture into the prepared pan and even out.

7. Place the cake into the oven and bake 75 minutes or until the sides break away from the pan.

8. Remove the cake from the oven and let cool in the pan 10 minutes.

9. Remove the cake from the pan and cool on a rack until ready to slice and serve.

ABBEY CRUMB CAKE

(makes 1 cake)

Perhaps a perfect dinner should end with a perfectly textured dessert. This crumble cake is unlike most others as the "crumble" is indeed the whole cake, from the top layer to the body of the cake. So delicate is the crumble texture of this cake, that it must be sliced as soon as it leaves the oven.

The crumble nature of this cake is accomplished by using finely ground almonds and yellow cornmeal, both products always available to the abbey cook. Another interesting fact regarding the texture of this cake is that unlike others of the same genre, when you place it in the pan, you do not pat it down. As it bakes, the immense heat from the oven brings everything together.

Upon the presentation of this cake to the guests, the footman would spoon a little heavy cream on the plate (unwhipped) and then place the slice on the plate. This made the cake easier to eat as the moisture from the heavy cream would soak into the bottom of the cake making it easier for the guest to get it onto the fork and up to his or her mouth. You don't want guests having crumbs all over their gowns or evening attire!

Ingredients needed to make Abbey Crumb Cake:

1 cup blanched almonds, finely ground
1½ cups flour
⅔ cup yellow cornmeal
½ cup sugar

1 tsp. finely grated lemon zest
2 egg yolks, beaten
½ cup butter, softened

Steps:

1. Preheat the oven to 375°F. Line the bottom of a 9-inch cake pan with parchment paper.

2. In a large bowl, whisk the almonds, flour, cornmeal, sugar, and zest until combined. Stir in the egg yolks and butter until the mixture starts to come together. You want it to be crumbly.

3. Sprinkle the mixture, by hand, into the prepared pan and even it out. Do not pat it down.

4. Place the cake into the oven and bake 40 minutes.

5. Remove the cake from the oven and carefully remove it from the pan.

6. While the cake is still warm, cut it into serving pieces and let it cool.

INDEX